Snap Shots

Bible

through the year!

**Bible reading for
8- to 11-year-olds**

© Scripture Union 2011

First published 2011

ISBN 978 1 84427 573 1

Scripture Union
207–209 Queensway, Bletchley, Milton Keynes, MK2 2EB, UK

SU England and Wales: www.scriptureunion.org.uk
SU Australia: www.scriptureunion.org.au
SU New Zealand: www.scriptureunion.org.nz
SU USA: www.scriptureunion.org

This Snapshots material has appeared in previously published issues of Snapshots.

Editorial team: Karen Evans, Helen Jones
Writers: Lizzie Green, Gill Hollis, Judith Merell, Doug Swanney, Di Tunnington
Artist: Colin Smithson
Layout: Helen Jones
Cover design: kwgraphicdesign
Printed by 1010 Printing International Ltd, China

Hi and welcome to

Did you know that God's not only with you all the time, but he wants to talk with you and listen to you, too? Using Snapshots is a great way to help you understand what God is saying through his Word, the Bible.

Each day Snapshots gives you a few Bible verses to read, something to think about or do, and a prayer idea!

If you can, find someone to read it with you. Find somewhere quiet, away from the TV.

Ask God to help you understand it before you start, then read the first part on the page.

Hear from God as you read the verses from the Bible, then read and act on the rest of the Snapshots bit.

Spend a bit of time talking with God, using the ideas on the page and your own ideas.

Finding your way round the Bible

The Bible is in two parts called the Old Testament and the New Testament.

Matthew is the first book in the New Testament – the second part of the Bible.

Matthew 1:21

Each book of the Bible is broken up into chapters. **Matthew** has 28 chapters and this verse is in the first chapter.

Matthew ①:21

Each chapter is split into verses, which are usually shown as very small numbers. This is verse 21.

Matthew 1:㉑

Use the Contents page in your Bible to find out where each book starts.

contents

Just about everything

1 January

Have you written all your Christmas thank you letters? Paul wrote letters to people who wanted to join together to praise God for Jesus.

Read Colossians 1:15–17.

See if you can crack the code then you will have the answer to the following questions! (Clue – take the first letter of each object.)

What was created by Jesus?

What was made for Jesus?

What does Jesus hold together?

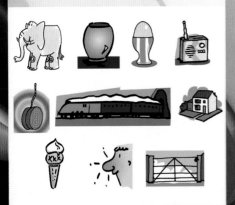

_ _ _ _ _ _ _ _ _ _ _ _ _!

Thank God that Jesus is so special.

Brought home!

2 January

Have you ever been lost? Fill in the faces to show how someone might feel when they are lost and then when they find someone they know.

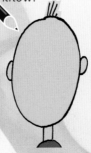

Read Colossians 1:18–20.

These verses tell us massive truths about Jesus.

See if you can fill in the gaps using the pictures as a clue.

Jesus is the head of his

_____, the church.

God made peace with us through Jesus' death on a _____.

So God can bring the whole _____ back to himself.

Enemies or friends?

3 January

How could an enemy become a friend again?

Read Colossians 1:21–23.

What made us God's enemies? Fill in the missing vowels.

E v _ l t h _ n g s w _
d _ d _ n d t h _ _ g h t

How did God make us his friends?

that
so
we
the cross could
uo his be
Jesus died friends

One day, God's friends will be holy, faultless and pure – that means totally good! Write "100% good" on the cross.

Dear God, thank you for sending Jesus to die for me so that I can be your friend. Help me to become the sort of friend you want me to be. Amen.

Out of this world

4 January

It is very sad when someone we care about dies, but because of Jesus we don't have to be scared.

Read Colossians 3:1–4.

If we really love Jesus, we will be with him in heaven one day.

Jesus is already there, with God, ready to welcome us.

It's hard to imagine what heaven will be like. Thinking of things we love might help.

Round the heart shape, draw pictures of three things in your life that you love.

Dear God, I love you. In my life I love _____

_____ and

_____.

Thank you that heaven will be full of your love. Amen.

Doing it God's way

5 January

Have you ever been specially chosen to do something? Why do you think you were picked?

Read Colossians 3:12–14.

God has chosen us because he loves us! So how should we behave?

Draw yourself in the white box and around your picture write how God wants you to behave.

Which of the things mentioned here do you find hardest? Ask God to help you.

When you get dressed, pretend that each piece of clothing you put on is something that will make you be the way God wants.

Tell others

6 January

What's your favourite hobby or sport? How much time do you spend doing it? Do you spend much time talking about it? When you really enjoy something, you often think and talk about it a lot of the time.

Read Colossians 3:15–17.

What does Paul say should fill our hearts and lives?

het essmgea bouta risthC

_____

Then what should we do?

aecht orsthe

_____

Who can you talk to about Jesus this week?

What else helps you remember Jesus?

snignig ot ogd

_____

itwh hankgivnigst

_____

What's love all about?

7 January

Do you agree with these thoughts?

Love is...

"A beautiful feeling in life that can be painful also." Jemima, aged 10

"Kind, caring and doesn't say hurtful words." Isabella, aged 9

Love isn't...

"Something mean." Kayla, aged 10

"Hatred or bullying." Gabby, aged 9

What do you love?

"The sea, drama, God, my family." Laura, aged 10

"Motorbikes." Riley, aged 9

What do you think God loves?

"Everyone and everything." Ellie, aged 10

"The people he made." Jason, aged 10

Write your own love thoughts here:

Meeting places

8 January

Have you ever met a very important person? People queue at concerts or film premieres to see someone famous. Usually there are loads of policemen, TV crews and press photographers, and sometimes there is a red carpet.

Read Exodus 19:1–3.

Where did Moses meet with God?

☐ A palace.

☐ The desert.

☐ A church.

☐ A mountain.

Mount Sinai was high, rocky and in the middle of the desert. No red carpets, crowds or cameras, but an awesome place for someone to meet an awesome God!

Thank you, God, that even though you are so mighty and awesome, you met with Moses, and you want to meet with us too. Amen.

Gentle power

A mother eagle is a very powerful bird that carries her baby eagles on her wings to help them learn to fly.

That's how our powerful God cares for his people, and that means us!

Read Exodus 19:3–6.

God wanted his people to obey and serve him.

What's something you know God wants you to do for him? Write it around the eagle. Make a plan now to do it. Ask God to help you.

Dear God, thank you for choosing me. Please help me to obey you and serve you today in everything I do. Amen.

Do you agree?

Often, when someone gets a new job, they sign a piece of paper called a contract. It tells them what they have to do, and when they sign it, they agree to do it. It was a bit like that with God and his people.

Read Exodus 19:7–8.

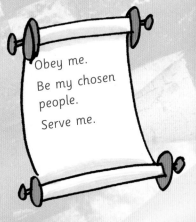

Obey me.
Be my chosen people.
Serve me.

If you want to do things God's way, there is a space at the bottom of this 'contract' for you to sign your name.

If you signed your name or you're thinking carefully about it, ask God to help you to do what it says.

Scrub up

No one turns up to a wedding in dirty, scruffy clothes! It's important to get ready for a special occasion.

Read Exodus 19:9–12.

True or false?
God would come in a thick cloud. **T/F**

It was because God is holy. **T/F**
The people had to wash their clothes before God came. **T/F**
It was because God is holy. **T/F**
The people were not allowed to touch or go near the mountain. **T/F**
It was because God is holy. **T/F**
(Answers on page 192.)

Holy means pure, total goodness. Only God is holy, but he wants us to be holy, too.

Holy God, I'm not good enough to come to you by myself. Thank you that Jesus comes with me and he is holy.

God is fearsome

What sorts of things make you go "Wow!"? Imagine a fantastic firework display, a terrific thunderstorm AND a huge orchestra playing really loudly, all at the same time! It was a bit like that when the people met with God.

Read Exodus 19:16–20.

What did the people see?
What did they hear?
What did they feel?

It was awesome! It was fearsome!

Thank you, God, that even though you are so holy and awesome, you want us to be your chosen people and serve you. Wow! That's amazing and...

Add some of your own words to tell God how you feel.

Meeting royalty

If you meet a king or queen:

DO call them "Your Majesty".

DON'T speak first.

DO bow or curtsey.

DON'T touch them.

Why? Because they are royal!

Draw yourself waiting to meet royalty.

Read Exodus 19:21–25.

Because God is so holy he has to make rules to protect his people. This shows how much he loves and cares for us. God is the King of kings but he still wants us to belong to him!

Something to make

Find some brightly coloured threads: red, blue, purple, green.

Red for powerful.
Blue for everlasting.
Purple for almighty.
Green for creator.

Tie them all together at one end, and weave a friendship bracelet. Wear it and think of what each colour represents and how great God is.

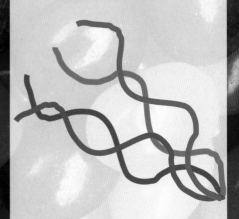

First place

When you watch a sports match you have to decide whose side you're on.

Read Exodus 20:1–6.

The Bible tells us that God is the only true God. He wants us to be 'on his side'. He should always be most important.

Around the number one, write or draw some things that are very important to you.

God should be our number one!

Write or draw inside the number one times when it's important to put God first. Then ask God to help you to do that.

Respect God's name

A lot of people say God's name in the wrong way – when they are surprised, or cross, or they can't think of anything else to say. What does God have to say about that?

Read Exodus 20:7.

Here are some ways to describe God:

- God is special
- God is powerful
- Everlasting – he always was and always will be
- Creator
- Almighty – he has all the power
- Lord – master or ruler

Ask God to help you use his name in the right way.

"R and R"

17 January

Have you ever heard anyone talking about "R and R"? It means "Rest and Relaxation", and it was all God's idea!

Read Exodus 20:8–11.

Even God had a rest after he had worked hard to create the world – it's very important!

Circle the things you enjoy doing at weekends, and then draw your favourite type of R and R.

sport...

reading...

church...

visiting...

partying...

movies...

games...

What does God say about our rest day? It should _____ to him (verse 10).

Think about how you could do that.

Respect your parents

18 January

No! Why should I?

Go away!

Have you ever said stuff like that to your mum or dad, or whoever cares for you?

The Bible tells us how we should act at home.

Read Exodus 20:12.

What does "respect" mean? Put a tick in the right boxes and a cross in the wrong ones:

☐ Being helpful.

☐ Doing what we want.

☐ Being polite.

☐ Answering back.

☐ Being rude.

☐ Being obedient.

☐ Being thankful.

☐ Being kind.

Dear God, I'm sorry for the times when I'm _____. Please help me to be _____. Amen.

Things not to do

19 January

Where might you see a sign like this?

Some rules are made for our protection, so that we don't harm ourselves or others.

Can you think of any other signs that give a warning? Draw them here.

Read Exodus 20:13–16.

Which verse is most important for you right now? Why?

God tells us not to do certain things because he knows what is best for us. Also, he knows that if we disobey him, other people will be hurt as well.

Be glad with what you have

20 January

Verses 1 to 17 of Exodus 20 tell us how to live God's way. To find out what they are often called, hold this page up to a mirror.

THE TEN COMMANDMENTS

Read Exodus 20:17.

Try these hand actions, or create your own, to remember these commandments.

 God is the only God.

 Respect God's name.

 God invented "R and R".

 Things not to do.

 Respect your parents.

 Be glad with what you have.

Thank God for his special rules.

Learn and remember

Have you ever tried remembering some verses from the Bible?

Read Psalm 1:1–3

> 1 God blesses those people who refuse evil advice and won't follow sinners or join in sneering at God.
>
> 2 Instead, the Law of the Lord makes them happy, and they think about it day and night.
>
> 3 They are like trees growing beside a stream, trees that produce fruit in season and always have leaves. Those people succeed in everything they do.
> Psalm 1:1–3

Read verse 3 again. The person who wrote this psalm says that people who turn away from evil and live their lives according to God's Law are just like evergreen trees growing beside a refreshing stream.

Draw an outline of a large tree. Inside it, write **Psalm 1:1–3** to learn and remember. Over the next week, read the first verse a couple of times. Then, a bit later, read the next verse as well.

By the end of the week, see if you can say all three verses from memory.

Don't be sheepish

Have you ever been lost? How did you feel? Meet Baa-rt.

He is a silly sheep who keeps wandering off and getting lost!

Find out what happened to a sheep in a story Jesus told.

Read Luke 15:1–7.

Why did Jesus tell this story?

☐ Because sheep were his favourite animals.

☐ To show that he loves us, even when we wander away from him like sheep.

☐ Because the people asked him to tell them a story.

(Psst!: Can you think of any other funny names for sheep?)

Lost!

Hide a coin and ask someone in your family to find it. How long do they take?

Read Luke 15:8–10.

When the woman in this story was hunting for her lost coin it wasn't a game, it was for real!

It's like that with us and God. If we do wrong things that don't please God, it's as if we are lost, like the coin. God wants us to turn away from the wrong things we do and come back to him.

The Bible tells us there's a celebration in heaven when that happens.

Hold a coin in your hand, think about today's story and then thank God that you are so important to him.

If only...

Sometimes, when we do something we shouldn't, we realise how silly we have been, but it's too late. Or is it?

Read Luke 15:11–16.

Draw the man and his two sons.

First mistake: the younger son should have waited till his father gave him the money.
Draw the younger son at work after he spent all of his dad's money.

Second mistake: he wasted all the money. What did the son need now?

Please God, help me to do things your way, not my way.

He got smart

Remember where we left the man's very hungry younger son in yesterday's story?

(Somewhere dirty and smelly. Yuk!)

Read Luke 15:17–19.

Cross out all the "pigs" and circle the words that are left:

1 Hepigscamepigstopigshispigs sensespigs

2 Hepigssaidpigshepigswouldpigs saypigssorrypigstopigshis pigsfather

Is there anything you've done that makes you feel bad when you think of God? What could you do about it?

Father God, please help me to see when I do things that are wrong. Please help me to be sorry for what I have done. Amen.

The loving father

What would you feel like if your friend had borrowed one of your toys and then broken or lost it?

How would the father react to seeing his son again?

Read Luke 15:20–27.

This story is often called "The lost son", but it could be called "The loving father". Which title do you think is best? Why?

Who does the father remind you of? Why?

Thank you, God, that you are like the loving father, always ready to forgive.

Try one of these with your family or friends:

• Read the story again and make up some sound effects.

• Act the story out.

The older brother

27 January

Sometimes we feel jealous of others.

Perhaps they have something we would like, or they are friends with someone we would like to be friends with. See how God treats someone who is jealous.

Read Luke 15:28–32.

When the younger brother came home, the older brother was jealous.

What did the father remind him about?

Put the words in the right places.

always	**me**
everything	**yours**
brother	**lost**	**found**

You are _____ here with _____ and _____ I have is _____. Your _____ was _____, but now he is _____.

Dear God, please help me not to be jealous of other people.
Please help me to remember how much you love me. Amen.

Singing to God

28 January

Have you ever wondered why we sing so much in church?

God loves it when we sing songs which tell him how we feel about him and how we feel about ourselves and his world.

Football supporters sing to celebrate the success of their team or to urge them to do great things. Christians have always sung songs to celebrate how wonderful God is and to praise him.

Mind you, some of the songs that are sung in church have poor tunes and not very good words. They may not always say what we want to say to God at the moment!

We can also learn bits of the Bible by singing them. The tune helps us to remember the words.

Have a go at remembering a Bible verse by humming a tune to it.

That's great!

29 January

What have you seen or heard or done this week that's been great?

Read Psalm 145:1–3.

King David wrote this psalm (you say it "sarm"). Write something he said about God in the speech bubble.

Read verse 2 again. How often did David thank God?

How often do you thank God?

The Psalms are songs and poems that are like prayers. They are still sung in many churches today. Lots of psalms say how wonderful God is – that's praise. In other psalms, the writer tells God he feels angry or needs help. We can talk to God about how we really feel.

What's the best way you can think of to praise God? Do it!

Never-ending story

30 January

Who told you about God? Was it someone older than you?

Down the centuries, people have told others about God. Parents tell their children, who tell their children, who…

Read Psalm 145:4–7.

Can you find three things people will say about God?

They will speak of God's…

_____ _____ and

_____.

Try to imagine yourself in 20 years!

How old will you be? Who might you be telling about God?

Ask God to help you tell others about him… now and in the future.

What's God like?

How would you describe God? These verses tell us what God's like. They don't say what God looks like because he can't be seen with our eyes.

Read Psalm 145:8–9.

Make up some actions to go with the words below. Then read the verses again, doing the actions.

Loving

Merciful

Slow to become angry/kind and patient

Full of constant love/always loving

Good to everyone

What do your friends think of God? Why not ask them! You could let them know what God is like by teaching them the actions you've made up.

What does God say to you through this psalm? What will you say to God about it?

Who's the king?

If you could choose someone to be king, who would it be? Why?

Read Psalm 145:10–13.

God is King of the world. He's the best!

Colour in the letters with a star to find out how long God will rule.

Why will God's people tell what he has done? (Verses 11 and 12 may help.)

What do you think is the best thing about knowing God?

Now think about what you want to say to God. Which words of praise will you use?

Who cares?

Have you ever fallen over at school or in the park? Who helped you up?

Read Psalm 145:14–21.

How does God look after the people who trust him?
Find the answers in the psalm.
What does God do if we…
are sad, in trouble or hurt (verse 14)?

_____

are hungry (verses 15–16)?

_____

need something (verse 19)?

_____

There's no problem we might have that God can't help us with.

Thank you, God, that you care about everyone, especially those in great need. Thank you that you care when I'm sad or hurt. Thank you that you give me all I need. You're amazing!

Tajikistan

Has your school ever closed because the heating was broken?
Last winter, many children in Tajikistan still went to school when there was no electricity for heating and the temperature was −17°C. That's as cold as inside a freezer!

Tajikistan is a country between China and Afghanistan. It is almost twice as big as Scotland and half the people who live there are aged under 14. Many people there are very poor, especially in the country areas.

In the summer it is very different – the temperature may be 38°C. That's when it's good to go to the countryside. Scripture Union in Tajikistan runs summer camps for children. They will have a great time and find out more about following Jesus.

where is too far?

4 February

Could you walk 40 kilometres?

How long would it take you to travel 40 kilometres by car? (You may need an adult to help you answer this.)

In today's story a government official travels 40 kilometres to ask Jesus for help.

Read John 4:46–54.

True or false?

The government official's daughter was very ill. **T/F**

Jesus said, "I'll come with you right away." **T/F**

The child got well at the same time that Jesus had promised the father. **T/F**

The whole family believed in Jesus. **T/F**

Jesus healed a child who was far away from him. **T/F**

(Answers on page 192.)

Nowhere is too far from Jesus' power.

Horizontal to vertical

5 February

Circle any of these actions if you have done them in the last two days:

run	**walk**	**cycle**
skate	**skateboard**	**dive**
jog	**somersault**	**climb**
skip	**lie down**	**swim**
dance	**hop**	**jump**

The man in today's story could only do one of these things. Which one?

Read John 5:1–9.

Draw how the man felt...
as he lay beside the pool.

when Jesus arrived.

when Jesus stopped to speak to him.

when he first walked.

Move around as much as you can and thank God for all the activities that you can do.

Like Father like Son

6 February

Have you ever heard someone say: "You look just like your mum/dad!"?

Or

"You do that just like your mum/dad does!"?

Jesus takes after his Father in heaven, not in his appearance but in his actions.

Read John 5:19–21.

In what ways does Jesus take after his Father, God?

Who does Jesus, the Son, give life to?

Think of at least three things that God does. Jesus does them, too!

God the Father, thank you that you can raise the dead and give new life. Jesus the Son, thank you that you do what God the Father does. Wow!

The amazing picnic

7 February

What kind of sandwich do you like best?

Cheese and pickle, strawberry jam, banana and honey, tuna mayonnaise, something else?

Read John 6:5–11.

Get counting!

- ☐ How many silver coins would be needed to buy bread for everyone?
- ☐ How many loaves did the boy have?
- ☐ And how many fish?
- ☐ How many men sat down?
- ☐ How many baskets of leftovers were there?
- ☐ And if half the men brought a wife and one child, how many people would there be in total?

(Answers on page 192.)

Thank you, Jesus, that you had the power to create a meal for so many people. Thank you for the good food that you provide for us.

A shore thing!

Imagine... a pleasant evening, a superb sunset, a boat trip across a lake. A strong breeze blows over the water. You and your friends have to row harder. The wind gets stronger, the boat rocks up and down until all of a sudden...

Read John 6:16–21.

Who came to the disciples?
Draw what you think they thought he was.

Why didn't they need to be afraid?

Read verse 21 again. It doesn't say "soon" or "later", but "immediately/suddenly they got to the shore/land".

That's faster than the speed of light!

Thank you, Lord, that you have the power to help us to cope when we are afraid.

What's a miracle?

A miracle is an amazing thing that is hard to explain and is not expected. They are sometimes called "mighty acts of God", "signs" or "wonders". When people saw them they were amazed. Miracles are performed by God, Jesus, or through ordinary people by the Holy Spirit's power.

Miracles point us to God (that's why they're sometimes called "signs"). They show us his power, like when, through Moses, he parted the Red Sea, or, through Elijah, raised people from the dead. Jesus showed God's love, care and power when he healed people or fed 5,000 hungry people with five loaves and two fish or stilled a storm.

All these things may seem amazing to us, but the Bible says that "nothing is impossible for God".

How many miracles in the Bible can you think of? Do you know of any miracles that have happened in your lifetime?

Miraculous sight

Shut your eyes for two minutes. What can you hear? What can you smell? What can you feel? What can you see? Life was like this for the blind man in our story.

Read John 9:1–7.

Can you find the nine bold words in this wordsearch in under two minutes?

Jesus, the **light** of the **world**, rubbed some **mud** on the **blind** man's **eyes**. He sent him to **wash** in the Pool of **Siloam**. He did as he was told and came back **seeing**.

S	J	E	S	U	S	W
I	W	A	S	H	E	O
L	I	G	H	T	E	R
O	E	Y	E	S	I	L
A	X	B	L	I	N	D
M	U	D	X	Y	G	Z

For the wondrous gift of eyes to see
The beauty of the world around me,
Thank you, Lord.

Can it be true?

How do you feel when a friend who's been ill gets better? No one seemed very pleased about the blind man.

Read John 9:13–23.

Who said what? Join the statements to the people who said them.

The Jewish leaders

The parents

The Pharisees

He can't be from God, he doesn't obey the law

We don't know how it happened

He can't have been blind

The Pharisees and leaders didn't think Jesus came from God because he didn't behave in the way they expected. (Remember that miracles were unexpected happenings. See page 25.)

Pray for anyone you know who doesn't realise who Jesus is.

Don't you get it?

"I don't get it!" Have you ever been told a joke but just not got it?

Read John 9:24–34.

The Pharisees had learnt a lot about God, but the blind man understood far more about who Jesus was, even though he'd only just met him!

Fill in the missing vowels to find out what he said.

_ w _ s b l _ n d _ n d n _ w
_ s _ _.
J _ s _ s c _ _ l d n _ t d _
_ n y t h _ n g _ n l _ s s
h _ c _ m _ f r _ m G _ d.

But the Pharisees still didn't "get it". Instead, what did they do?

T h _ y w _ _ l d n ' t l _ t
t h _ b l _ n d m _ n b _ c k
_ n t h _ s y n _ g _ g _ _

Are there things you don't "get" about Jesus? Ask him to help you understand.

Being blind

It sounds like a riddle: a blind man sees and sighted people become blind! How come?

Read John 9:35–41.

What did the man say to Jesus? Cross out the BLINDs.

BLINDLORDBLINDIBLINDPUTBLIND
MYBLINDFAITHBLINDINBLINDYOU.

What did the Pharisees ask? Cross out the SEEs.

SEEARESEEWESEEBLINDSEETOO?

The Pharisees refused to change their minds about Jesus even when they'd seen what he did. That's why Jesus said they were blind.

Think of three things you know about Jesus. How do they help you understand who he is? (You might need an adult you trust to help you with this.)

Read verse 38 again. If you really mean it, say what the man said and do what he did.

Sabbath stuff

The Bible talks a lot about the "Sabbath", but what is it?

The word "Sabbath" means "to cease", "to stop".

One of the Ten Commandments is about the Sabbath. See if you can find it in **Deuteronomy 5**. God was the first to have a day of rest. See **Genesis 2:2**.

The Sabbath is a holy day, which is where we get our word "holiday"!

The Pharisees made up lots of extra rules to stop people working on the Sabbath.

They said people must not carry things and doctors must not heal people. They said Jesus was breaking the law when he made sick people well on the Sabbath. Jesus challenged this idea! Check out **Matthew 12:11**.

Having a day of rest is God's idea! I wonder if you have a "Sabbath"-type day?

Who's the boss?

The people of Israel were taken away to Babylon as prisoners.

God had warned them it would happen if they worshipped other gods, but they ignored him and kept worshipping idols (pretend gods) made of wood and stone. They'll be more about this on 19 February.

Read Isaiah 44:6–8.

In the speech bubble write what God says about himself in verse 6.

Find a time and a place where you won't annoy anyone and shout out, "The Lord Almighty has this to say: 'I am the first, the last, the only God; there is no other god but me'."

Lord God, help me to be true to you because you're the only true God.

Who worships wood?

Have you ever made something that you were really proud of? What did you do with it?

What about the carpenter in today's reading?

Read Isaiah 44:13–19.

Circle two things the carpenter made with his wood.

a fire   a house

a boat   an idol

What does the man say to his wooden idol? (Cross out the wrong answers.)

"You are my god – save me!"

"Aren't I clever?"

"It'll make a nice present."

Which is greater, the wood or the one who made it?

Dear God, please help me to worship you and nothing else.

Remembering

Do you ever use notes to remind you of something important? What does God want you to remember?

Read Isaiah 44:21–23.

Finish God's reminders to you.

God didn't just create us, he loves and forgives us, too!

Read verse 22 again.

In the cloud write something you want to say sorry for.

Now picture God blowing the cloud away.

How does that make you feel?

Write your feelings in the sun

Who knows?

18 February

Do you know what you will do next week?

Are you sure? What does God say about the future?

Read Isaiah 44:24–28.

Astrologers make horoscopes. Are you ever tempted to read your horoscope? Look at verse 25 again.

Who knows more about the future than astrologers and fortune-tellers?

Cyrus was the king of Babylon, the one who had made prisoners of God's people. In verse 28, God tells Cyrus what Cyrus will do! And history shows that Cyrus did it.

Thank you, God, that you are the greatest. The strongest leaders are not as great as you.

You know what lies ahead.

Help me to always trust you.

Prisoners and prophets

19 February

In 587 BC, King Nebuchadnezzar of Babylon invaded the city of Jerusalem. He burned God's temple and took the people over 1,000 kilometres away to Babylon, in the area that is now Iraq. This is called "the exile" because the people were forced to live in exile, away from their own country.

Isaiah, one of God's prophets, told the people that God had not forgotten them. He said that even though they were living in a foreign country, God was there, and they should worship God, not the foreign idols.

Ezekiel, another prophet, explained that God let the exile happen because his people had turned away to follow other gods. Ezekiel gave God's people hope for a better future.

Prove it!

20 February

"Go on then, prove it!" Has anyone ever said that to you?

God challenges the people who worship idols to prove that idols are better than he is.

Read Isaiah 45:18–25.

So – how many true gods are there (verse 22)?

One day everyone will know this. How will they show it (verse 23)?

God longs for everyone to turn to him. Think of two friends who don't know God, then pray this prayer:

Dear God, please help
_____ and
_____ to see how great you are. Help them to turn to you and learn to trust you.

How can you help your friends discover how great God is?

Show us!

21 February

When you were younger, did you have a favourite teddy or doll?

Think about the difference between what it can do and what you can do!

Read Isaiah 46:3–9.

Use the verses to fill in the table:

What God does	What idols can't do

Read verse 5 again.

What do you think? Is there anyone else like God?

Tell him your thoughts. Be honest.

Draw a picture of some things that God has made or done.

Write across the top of it, "He is the only God."

Listening to God

Sometimes it takes practice to tune in to what God's saying. Here are some ways to try.

The world around you

Starry nights, the wild ocean, little creatures... When you notice these things, think what they tell you about God.

The Bible

It's the story of God and his people, but it's more than just words on pages. Open your spirit as well as your eyes when you read. Listen for what God is saying to you.

Listening prayers

Sit quietly and let God tell you things, in your mind. Or listen while you walk, run, or swim, asking God to communicate with you.

People

God lives in his people. Watch out for others saying or doing things for God.

It's for you!

Do you ever get text messages or emails?

There weren't any phones or computers in Bible times, so people sent letters.

We're looking at a letter that Paul wrote to Christians living in Philippi, Greece.

Read Philippians 2:1–4.

Where do you live?
In _____ (place),
_____ (country).

This letter is for you, too! Check out verses 3 and 4, and then finish the letter on this scroll.

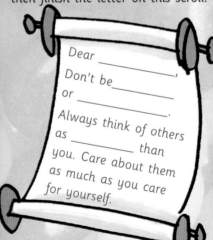

Dear _____,
Don't be _____
or _____.
Always think of others
as _____ than
you. Care about them
as much as you care
for yourself.

Dear God, help me to care for others. Amen.

The Servant King

24 February

Kings and queens are looked after by lots of servants. They have pages, footmen, butlers, chefs, private secretaries, ladies-in-waiting and... the list goes on and on! But Jesus, the greatest king ever, became a servant himself. Wow!

Read Philippians 2:5–11.

Which verse tells us about Jesus becoming a servant or slave?
Verse _____.

Circle the words that describe Jesus.

proud   humble
boastful   obedient
selfish   put others first

Do the words that you haven't circled remind you of anything?
Check your answers in the prayer below.
Check back to yesterday's Bible verses.

Please, God, help me to be like Jesus – humble, obedient, and putting other people first.
Amen.

Be a star!

25 February

If you are asked to make your bed and tidy your room, what do you say? Be honest!

☐ Do I have to?
☐ Why should I?
☐ It's not fair! My friends don't have to tidy their rooms.
☐ I'll do it now.
☐ I suppose I could do it later if I have to.

Read Philippians 2:12–16.

Which of these is correct? Circle the right one. (Verse 14 will help!)
Do everything without whispering or shouting.
Do everything without laughing or joking.
Do everything without complaining or arguing.

Draw a picture showing what verse 15 tells us to be. Can you colour it in gold or silver?

Find a torch and shine it on a wall or ceiling. Look at the light on the wall and think what it means to shine for Jesus.

VIP

Did you know that the letters VIP stand for Very Important Person? Who do you know who is very important? Why are they important? Is it because of something they do, or have, or are they in charge of something?

Read Philippians 3:8–11.

Paul wrote this letter to the people of Philippi. Who does he say is the most important of all?

Cross out the wrong answers and underline the right one:

rich people

famous people

clever people

Jesus

Dear God, I want Jesus to be my VIP. Help me to get to know him better as I read the Bible, talk with him and become more like him in the way I behave.
Amen.

Keep going!

What do all these sports have in common?

(The answer is on page 192.)

Read Philippians 3:12–14.

True or false? Being in a sports team isn't always easy, but we need to keep going.

True or false? Following Jesus' way isn't always easy, but we need to keep going.

How do we keep going? What can we do that will help us to follow Jesus' way?
Run on the spot for 60 seconds. Was that hard? Are you out of breath? Now finish this prayer.

Dear God, following Jesus' way is sometimes hard, especially when I'm _____.
Please help me to keep going and not give up.

Wow!

What makes you think, "Wow!"?

Write or draw it/them here:

Read Philippians 3:20–21.

Usually people are citizens of the country where they live, but Christians are citizens of heaven as well! One day, all people who are God's friends will be with him in heaven for ever.

Does that make you think, "Wow!"?

Read verse 20 again. While you are waiting for Jesus to come from heaven, do you need God's help to be a star, or to keep going? Talk to him about it now.

Are you a sheep?

In the Bible, God often describes his people as sheep, and those that lead them as shepherds.

Read Ezekiel 34:1–4.

Do you think the leaders of Israel sound selfish or caring?

_____

Do they take things from the sheep or give them a good life?

_____

Are the leaders looking after the sick sheep or ignoring them?

_____

Do they find the lost ones or treat them cruelly?

_____

If you were a leader and God said you were like this, how would you feel? Draw a picture or write some words in the sheep to show this.

Listen up!

Read Ezekiel 34:7–10.

God says he will punish the leaders for not looking after the "sheep". (Remember the sheep were really the people.) What are the punishments?

☐ God will give them more sheep to look after.

☐ God will rescue the sheep himself.

☐ God will give the shepherds a reward.

☐ God will never let the leaders be shepherds again.

☐ God will do nothing.

Look back to yesterday and remind yourself of the things the leaders did to deserve this punishment.

God is the Lord, the living God (verse 8). That means he is the same today as he has always been. Thank God now for all that he has done for his people down through history.

(Psst! What do you get if you cross a sheep with a kangaroo? A woolly jumper!)

Lost, not forgotten

How many sheep can you find?

God has promised to find all the lost sheep, wherever they are.

Read Ezekiel 34:11–16.

There's a hidden meaning in these words.

The "dark, disastrous/miserable day" was when the people of Israel were taken away as prisoners by the Babylonians. God says he'll bring them back.

Put the right words in the gaps.

lost   heal   safety

God promises to…

Let them graze in _ _ _ _ _ _.

Look for those that are _ _ _ _.

_ _ _ _ those that are sick.

Messing things Up

3 March

God has spoken to the leaders, now he turns to the sheep, his people. What has God noticed about them?

Read Ezekiel 34:17–19.

More hidden meanings! What do you think "trampling grass" and "muddying the water" for others means? Talk about it this week with an older person you trust.

When God created the world there was enough food and water for everyone. Today, not everyone gets a fair share, and some people are hungry and thirsty all the time.
That's not the way God wants it.

Ask God to show you if there is any way you can help others get what they need.

Find out if your church or school helps people in need.

security guaranteed

4 March

Unfairness won't last for ever.

Read Ezekiel 34:20–25.

Unjumble the words:
God will separate the _ _ _ _ _ _ tngrso from the _ _ _ _ kewa.
He will separate the _ _ _ _ dgoo from the _ _ _ dba.
He will give the people a _ _ _ _ nigK like his servant _ _ _ _ _ vidDa.

God kept this promise and sent a king like David to rescue all the people. Who was it? Look at **Matthew 1:1** and write his name here.

Thank you, God, that in heaven everything will be fair. Thank you that you sent a good shepherd to rescue us all. Amen.

Did you know? King David was a shepherd when he was young!

could you want more?

5 March

The Temple was built on Mount Zion in the capital city of Jerusalem. It was the most important place in all of Israel, sometimes called God's sacred hill or holy mountain (verse 26).

Read Ezekiel 34:26–31.

Let these pictures remind you of the things God promised his people in this passage

Enough

Protection from

Respect from

But the best thing of all is in verse 31.

These people were terrified of wild animals and fighting enemies. Find some paper and write down or draw some things that frighten you.

Hold the paper while you talk to God about those things. Ask for his protection and thank him for being your good shepherd.

Without God

6 March

What's it like when people don't take any notice of God?

Read Psalm 14:1–3

Can you unjumble the words? People who say, "There is no God!" are:

les throws _____.

leah rests _____.

cot purr _____.

rule c _____.

People who search for God and worship him are:

i sew _____.

What can you do to help people to be wise and not foolish?

Pray about some of the bad things you've seen on TV or in the newspaper today.

Don't give up!

Are you someone who keeps on asking for something, or do you give up easily?

Read Luke 11:5–8.

Imagine what it's like to be fast asleep at midnight, then there's a loud banging at the door. God isn't like the friend who'd gone to bed! God is never lazy and he doesn't need to sleep. But sometimes he doesn't say "Yes" straight away.

Why do you think Jesus told this story?
Crack the code, using codebreaker 1 on page 48.

L F F Q   P O   B T L J O H

_____

Have you been praying for someone or something, but God hasn't answered yet?

Write it in the white box, then keep on asking.

Fantastic presents!

What has been the best present you have ever received? What made it the best?

Read Luke 11:9–13.

On one plate draw the two things the son asks for.

On the second plate draw the two things that even a bad father wouldn't give his child, and then cross them out.

What does God, who is better than even the best father, want to give us?

_____

The Holy Spirit makes us more like Jesus.

Thank God that he wants to give us good things. Ask God to make you more like Jesus, so you know what to pray for and how to please him.

Don't worry!

9 March

Have you read the Mr Men books? Do you remember Mr Worry? Even when all Mr Worry's problems had been solved, he worried about having nothing to worry about!

Read Luke 12:22–28.

In the thought bubble draw or write what Jesus said people worry about. Then add other things you worry about. Jesus said there was no point in worrying because God cares for us, and God does everything well.

Thank God for looking after you. Then thank God that you don't need to worry about what you drew in the thought bubble.

Prayer time

10 March

When you were younger did you put your hands together when you prayed? (Leaders sometimes get little kids to do that to stop them fidgeting with their hands when their group is praying!)

Do you think there's a right way to pray or one that works better than others?

Jesus prayed in different ways at different times.

Match the verses to the description.

Mark 14:35   Looking up to heaven

Mark 6:41   Throwing himself on the ground/ kneeling

Luke 23:46   Shouting, crying in a loud voice

Jesus also suggested we pray quietly in our room (**Matthew 6:6**).

How do you like to pray?

It's not the way we do it that counts, it's all about God and being with him. Why not try a different way of praying this week?

Where's your treasure?

11 March

Imagine your house is flooded, but your family and pets are safe. If you could save just one of your possessions, what would you choose?

Read Luke 12:29–34.

Circle the valuable things which can't go rusty or be destroyed or stolen – things that last for ever.

wisdom   bike   faith

love   doing God's work

self-control   jewellery

TV   goodness

clothes   trust

computer   PlayStation

pictures   kindness   mobile

following Jesus   skateboard

Now join those things to the treasure chest.

(Psst! Jesus isn't saying that people should sell everything they own. But we need to realise that possessions won't last. Pleasing God is more important.)

The holy throne

12 March

When you think about heaven, what do you think about? John had a dream, or vision, about heaven which he wrote down in Revelation, the last book of the Bible.

Read Revelation 4:1–6.

Try to picture this. What do you think are the most amazing things John writes about?

Sometimes we think holy means quiet and serious, but not here! God's holiness is here described as brightness and thunder: it must have been an amazing sight! Heaven certainly isn't quiet either!

Think big and bright thoughts as you thank God for heaven. Use as many colours and exciting words as you can.

Holy singing!

Do you remember your dreams? Sometimes dreams can be amazing things where we can see extraordinary creatures and people. The last book of the Bible is a set of dreams that God gave to John and he passed on to us.

Read Revelation 4:7–11.

What an amazing picture of heaven John saw in his vision! Could you draw this?

Find one of your favourite songs on CD or, if you play an instrument, find your favourite piece of music.

Using the music you found, worship God in prayer by listening, singing along or playing your favourite piece of music. If you want to make up your own song, use the words in verses 8 and 11, even if you find them a bit hard to understand.

chosen people

Peter wrote a letter to Christians who were scattered in many places. Sometimes they found it hard to do the right thing. So he begins his letter by reminding them of a few good things.

Read 1 Peter 1:1–2.

Fill in the gaps:
The people were _____ by God.
God's Spirit had made them

_____.

Peter prays for the people with the last line of verse 2. Draw someone in this square whom you would like to have God's peace. Then pray for them.

Think about what it means to be chosen by God. How does it make you feel?

More about treasure!

What things are special to you? Draw your treasures here.

Read 1 Peter 1:3–4.

Use Codebreaker 1 on page 48 to work out some of the good things that God has given us.

OFX MJGF.

_____.

B IPQF UIBU MJWFT PO.

_____.

SJDI CMFTTJOHT TUPSFE VQ JO IFBWFO.

_____

_____.

What blessings do you think God has stored up for you? Thank him for them.

Testing times!

This work is too hard for me!

I don't want to go to school.

Things are unhappy at home.

Do you ever think any of these things? We all have hard times sometimes – Peter knew that!

Read 1 Peter 1:5–7.

What is our faith like?

It is more than _____.

Colour in the dotted shapes.

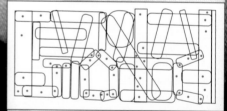

Gold is tested to prove that it is pure by being heated to a very high temperature. How do you feel when your trust in Jesus is put to the test?

Ask God to help you when things get hard for you.

Loving Jesus

17 March

Underline the things you can see. Circle the things you can't see.

electricity   trees   air
cars   love   people
Holy Spirit   Jesus

Read 1 Peter 1:8–9.

Use Codebreaker 1 on page 48 to work out what Peter says about our faith in Jesus.

XF EP OPU TFF KFTVT CVU XF KPWF IJN

_____

_____

After Jesus had come alive again, he praised people who did not see him but had faith. Turn to **John 20:24–29**.

Who in this story only believed in Jesus after he saw him? _____

_____

What did he say when he realised it was Jesus? _____

_____

Jesus was talking about us when he spoke about people who can't see him but have faith!

Living to please

18 March

Do you sometimes find it hard to do the right thing?

Read 1 Peter 1:13–15.

Find these six words that Peter uses in this wordsearch.

alert   hope
Christ   holy
desires   obedient

Then use the leftover letters to finish the sentence.

Be holy __ __ __ __ __ __ __ __ __ __

A	S	E	R	I	S	E	D
L	C	H	R	I	S	T	I
E	N	H	O	L	Y	A	L
R	L	Y	O	P	U	D	O
T	N	E	I	D	E	B	O

What does it mean to be holy? It must mean to be like God! But how is that possible? Does it mean letting God help you to live in a way that pleases him? Or does it mean really trying to do what you know is right? Or both?

Decide in your mind to please God. Then ask him to help you.

Rescued by the cross

If we were stuck at sea a lifeboat might come and rescue us. If our home was on fire we might be rescued by fire-fighters.

Read 1 Peter 1:18–20.

What danger are we in?

_____
(Put verse 18 in your own words.)
Who rescued us?_____

Think about Jesus, who rescued us by being willing to die. What does Peter say can't rescue us and doesn't last?

In this cross shape, write a prayer thanking Jesus for being willing to die on the cross.

Three cheers!

When do you cheer? When your team wins? When you come to the end of a boring journey? When it's pizza for tea?

Read Psalm 118:1–4.

The psalms were written as songs, and they often have a chorus that is repeated. Write down the chorus from this part of **Psalm 118**:

_____

Make a Cheer God Banner!
Use a long, thin sheet of paper. Write on it the words of the chorus from **Psalm 118** – or put them in your own words. Decorate.
Now you can wave your cheers to God.

Wave your banner as you thank God for all he has done.

Use your Cheer God Banner each day this week when you talk with God.

A problem shared...

21 March

What makes you feel really fed up? What do you do about it?
Grumble? Cry? Bite your nails? Or do you ask God to help?

Read Psalm 118:5–9.

People say a problem shared is a problem halved. If you have a bad problem, it's good to talk to a grown-up you trust. Sometimes even powerful people don't have the answer.
But God does.

If God is on your side, what does that mean?

Today or tomorrow, try to remember the words of verse 6 at least three times.

(Psst! Do you have a friend with a problem? Would it help them to share it with you?)

Dear God, help me never to forget that you are always with me!

Attack!

22 March

Who do you go to for help when things are going wrong?
The psalm writer was having a lot of trouble! His enemies were closing in. What could he do?

Read Psalm 118:10–14.

The enemies were gone! Who had defeated them?
The psalm writer/the Lord/another army/a swarm of bees
This part of the psalm has a refrain (or bit that's repeated often). Write it here:

_____

_____

Try remembering it when you need help.

(If you are worried about something really big, tell someone you can trust. Don't keep it to yourself.)

Pray for Christians whose lives are in danger from violent enemies, just because they love God. Ask God to save and help them.

Shout it out

23 March

How long does it take you to read four or five Bible verses? A few minutes? The psalm writer's problems lasted a lot longer and, usually, so do ours.

Read Psalm 118:15–18.

What were the people in the tent shouting?

Write inside the speech bubble what they said.

The writer has had a very hard time, but with God's help he's got through. What's he going to do now? (Verse 17.)

Thank God that he is the one who can sort out problems, even yours.

Don't forget to wave your banner!

Praise God!

24 March

Where do you go to be with others who want to praise God? The psalm writer went to the Temple.

Read Psalm 118:19–23.

Read verse 22 again. The capstone was the most important stone in the temple building. This psalm was written hundreds of years before Jesus, but Jesus took these words and used them to mean himself. (Check out **Matthew 21:42**.)

The Jewish and Roman leaders didn't accept Jesus. They rejected him, but he turned out to be the most important person of all. Write his name in the big stone.

Think of three great things that Jesus did, then praise him. Remember, you can praise God anywhere!

Codebreaker 1

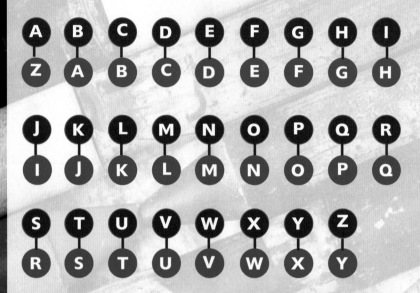

A	B	C	D	E	F	G	H	I
Z	A	B	C	D	E	F	G	H

J	K	L	M	N	O	P	Q	R
I	J	K	L	M	N	O	P	Q

S	T	U	V	W	X	Y	Z
R	S	T	U	V	W	X	Y

Codebreaker 2

	1	2	3	4	5
A	A	B	C	D	E
B	F	G	H	I	J
C	K	L	M	N	O
D	P	Q	R	S	T
E	U	V	W	X	Y

Let's celebrate

25 March

Smile, sing, shout, clap, jump, dance, wave a flag! How many ways can you celebrate?

Read Psalm 118:24–29.

Nowadays lots of people think that celebrating only means getting drunk. No one was drunk in this psalm. Instead, they were bubbling over with praise to God. Try and picture what they were doing.

An old song about favourite things begins:

"Raindrops on roses and whiskers on kittens..."

Can you continue, with the things that make you happy? Then you can sing it as a song of praise to God. It doesn't matter if it doesn't rhyme! Wave your banner as you sing.

Obey God's rules

26 March

Your parents insist that you must not ride your bike on the busy main road because:

☐ They like inventing new rules.

☐ They are spoil sports.

☐ They love you and want you to stay safe.

God has given us special rules because he loves us and wants us to live happily together. Use codebreaker 1 on page 48 to find out what they are called.

UIF UFO DPNNBOENFOUT

_____

_____

Read Deuteronomy 6:1–3.

How long should the people obey God's rules (verse 2)?

What did God promise to his people (verse 3)?

Father God, thank you that you care enough to tell us how to live. Help us to obey you.

(Psst! The name Deuteronomy means "second law". God's law is first recorded in Exodus.)

Love God

How would you describe what love is? Cross out the words that you think are not part of love.

Love is...

patient

thoughtless

short-tempered

willing to help

caring

sharing

generous

big-headed

good at listening

kind

Read Deuteronomy 6:4–5.

Can you fill in the missing words? Love the Lord your God with all your _ _ _ _ _ , with all your _ _ _ _ , and with all your _ _ _ _ _ _ _ _.
Deuteronomy 6:5

Please God, help me to love you with everything that's in me and with everything I have.

Off by heart

How do you remember important information?

☐ Write it on the back of your hand.

☐ Scribble it on a sticky note.

☐ Tie a knot in your hankie.

☐ Something else.

Read Deuteronomy 6:6–9.

The Bible words are thousands of years old. If God was telling us this now he might say it like this:

"Never forget these **rules** that I am giving you today. Teach them to your children. Repeat them when you are at home and when you are **at school**, when you are **relaxing** and when you are doing your **homework**. Tie them on your arms as **wristbands** and wear them on your **baseball caps** as a reminder. Use them as **computer screen savers** and write them on your **notebooks**."

Lord, help me to learn and remember your special rules for a happy life.

Thanks, God!

Have you seen any award ceremonies where the winners make thank you speeches? When good things happen it's important to thank the people who helped them happen.

Read Deuteronomy 6:10–13.

Can you find six things that would be ready and waiting for the Israelites in the country that God was leading them to?

L _ _ _

C _ _ _ _ _ /T _ _ _ _

H _ _ _ _ _

W _ _ _ _

V _ _ _ _ _ _ _

O _ _ _ _   O _ _ _ _ _ _ _

(Answers on page 192.)

What do you think the Israelites should do once they reach the new country that God has promised to them?

Think about some of the people who have helped and guided you. Remember to thank God for them – and perhaps you could say thank you to them too.

Trust, don't test

Has anyone ever said to you, "I don't believe you can do it! Prove it!"? Sometimes our friends doubt our ability and put us to the test.

Read Deuteronomy 6:14–19.

In the desert at Massah, God's people asked God to prove that he could help them. Look up Exodus 17:3–7 and then draw what the people complained about.

Check out the verses in Deuteronomy again. Is it right to test God? Yes/No

Think about some of the things that God has done for you. Ask God to strengthen your trust in him so that you don't have to ask him to prove his power.

Future hope

31 March

Do your parents tell you stories about when they were young? Find out what Moses told the parents long ago to tell their children.

Read Deuteronomy 6:20–25.

In these verses, what do you think is the most amazing thing God did for these people?

☐ Rescued them from slavery.

☐ Sent plagues on their enemies.

☐ Brought them safely through the desert to a new land.

☐ Gave them his laws to obey.

What a life! They complained and even wanted to go back to slavery, but God never gave up on them. God proved that he is

GBJUIGVM _ _ _ _ _ _ _ _ .

(Use Codebreaker 1 on page 48.)

Lord, thank you for watching over us in the past. Please be close to us in the future.

Reminders of Jesus

1 April

Which special days do you remember in your home or country? How do you celebrate? Jewish people celebrate the Passover by eating a meal together. Passover is a celebration of the time when God rescued his people from Egypt.

Read Mark 14:12–16, 22–26.

Where did Jesus eat the special meal? Tick the right box:

☐ At home.

☐ On the Mount of Olives.

☐ In an upstairs room.

Jesus gave the festival a double meaning.

What did the bread and wine represent?

This is_____.

In many churches, people still use bread and wine to remind them of Jesus. The service may be called communion or breaking of bread. What's it called in your church?

Lord Jesus, help me to see how awesome Jesus' actions were. Help me to understand what they mean for me.

Jesus knew Peter

🗒 **2 April**

Best friends stick together when bad things happen. Right? See what Jesus said his friends would do when things got tough for him.

Read Mark 14:27–31.

Fill in the speech bubbles.

> I will never _____.

> Before the cock crows twice, you will _____.

Who do you think was right about what Peter would do, Jesus or Peter? (Find out on 6 April.)

Jesus knew Peter really well, but it didn't stop him loving him.

Jesus knows exactly what we're like and it doesn't stop him loving us either!

Lord Jesus, I praise you because you didn't chicken out of dying for us all, even though you knew your friends would let you down.

Jesus' prayer

🗒 **3 April**

Have you ever fallen asleep and missed something important?

Read Mark 14:32–42.

How loyal were Jesus' friends? Mark it on the line.

not interested   quite faithful   totally loyal

_____

How loyal are you to Jesus? Mark it in a different colour.

This was probably the worst moment of Jesus' life so far.

Find these unhappy words in the wordsearch:

distress, anguish, sorrow, crushes, suffering, weak, sinful, betray.

```
S F A T H E R N O T
O I C R U S H E S A
R W N H W A T I W N
R S U F F E R I N G
O A N T U B A U T U
W W H A T L Y K O I
U W D I S T R E S S
B E T R A Y A N T H
```

What did Jesus pray? Make a sentence with the leftover letters.

_ _ _ _ _ _ / _ _ _ / _ _ _ _ /
_ / _ _ _ _ / _ _ _ / _ _ _ _ /
_ _ _ / _ _ _ .

Arrested!

4 April

Have you seen arrests in films? Often the suspected criminal argues, fights or tries to run away. Jesus was different.

Read Mark 14:43–50.

Who came with the crowd to arrest Jesus?

Which part of the story do you think is the saddest? Why?

Say aloud the question Jesus asks in verse 48.

Did U have 2 come with and 2 capture me?

Does anyone answer? Yes/No

What do you think is the answer?

_____

Lord Jesus, all your friends let you down. Please forgive me when I let you down, too.

Evidence?

5 April

Jesus was always good but his enemies wanted to prove he was a bad man. Could they?

Read Mark 14:53–56.

Unjumble the sentences:

council to evidence. tried The find some

_____

_____

evidence. could They not any find told witnesses lies. Many

_____

_____

did Their agree. stories not

_____

Lord Jesus, were you scared when these things happened? Were you angry? Please help me to be like you and trust God whatever happens.

To understand more about why Jesus died, look at page 56.

Spot the lies

When were you last tempted to tell a lie? When did you actually tell one? Why? Spot the whoppers Peter told in this reading.

Read Mark 14:66–73.

How many times did Peter deny he knew Jesus?

Why would he do that? Tick the reason:

☐ He didn't like Jesus.

☐ He was scared.

☐ He always told lies.

☐ He forgot.

Can you remember something Jesus said about this? (Look back to April 2.)

Why do you think Peter cried? Write or draw what he might be thinking.

Think of some times you might be tempted to tell a lie. Imagine Jesus standing beside you.

Lord, help me to be truthful, especially when it comes to being faithful to you.

Go with the flow!

Do you ever "go with the flow", going along with others for an easy time?

Read Mark 15:6–15.

Underline the right word:

Pilate was the Roman governor.

He gave the Jews a favour every **Christmas/Passover/Easter.**

Barabbas was a **liar/robber/murderer.**

The chief priests were **jealous/frightened/angry.**

Pilate wanted to be **honest/popular/strong.**

Why did the crowd ask for Barabbas instead of Jesus?

How did the chief priests stir up the crowd?

Write what they said.

Why did they do this? (Look at verse 10.)

Sacrifices

8 April

In Old Testament times, God told his people to offer him sacrifices. Sometimes sacrifices were food, like flour, grain or bread. Sometimes it involved killing animals or birds. The Hebrew word for sacrifice is "zebach" (you say it "ze-bok") which means "slaughtered animal".

Some sacrifices were to say thanks to God for the blessings he gave them. Some were to say sorry for doing wrong. It was the job of the priests to kill the animals and offer the blood as a sacrifice to "pay for" the sins of all the people. That way the people weren't punished – the animal took their punishment for them.

Now we don't need to kill an animal to "pay for" what we do against God. When Jesus died on the cross, he became the sacrifice for us as his blood was poured out and he took our punishment. To find out more read **Hebrews 9:13–14.**

Beat him!

9 April

How do you feel when people laugh at you or criticise you? Jesus knows what that's like. Find out how he knows.

Read Mark 15:16–20.

Jesus didn't look or act like an earthly king. Kings wore purple robes, but the soldiers didn't believe Jesus was a king.

Colour Jesus' robe purple and draw the crown of thorns on his head. Draw a stick in the soldier's hand.

Jesus said that when we're kind to those who are badly treated, it's like being kind to him. What would Jesus think about people being teased and put down?

King Jesus, thank you that you understand how I feel when people are unkind to me.

Jesus is crucified

10 April

Have you ever seen a film about Jesus' death? What was the worst bit?

Read Mark 15:21–32.

What did the sign above the cross say?
T_ _ K_ _ _ o_ t_ _ J_ _ _

Did Jesus get treated like a king? What did people shout at him? Unjumble the letters:
omce onwd fmor hte oscsr
aevs oeylufsr

_____

_____

_____

Why didn't Jesus do what they said? (Not sure? Look again at 8 April.)

When Jesus died he was dying in your place.
Talk to God about what happened to Jesus and what it means to you.

A dramatic finish!

11 April

After hours of waiting, suddenly it's all action! As you read, imagine yourself there.

Read Mark 15:33–39.

What could you hear and see? Here are some clues:

Four people spoke. Who were they? What did they say?

What might you have said if you'd been there?

One person realised something very important. Use Codebreaker 2 on page 48 to find out what it was.

D5 B3 B4 D4 / C3 A1 C4 /
D3 A5 A1 C2 C2 E5 / E3 A1 D4 /
D5 B3 A5 / D4 C5 C4 /
C5 B1 / B2 C5 A4

Pray for someone you know who doesn't yet realise that Jesus really is the Son of God.

Jesus is buried

Are you good at spotting what has to be done before someone tells you?

Read Mark 15:42–47.

Think about Joseph of Arimathea.

What was his job?

What was he like?

What did he ask for?

What did he do?

Who watched him? Draw them in the picture.

Joseph was good, brave and practical. Ask God if there's anything practical he wants you to do for him.

(Psst! Jews always hurried to get their jobs done before the Sabbath, so they could have a rest when it came.)

He's alive!

Some people say Easter eggs are for new life. Others say the eggs represent the stone at the tomb. Find out about both in this reading.

Read Mark 16:1–8.

Imagine: an Easter egg so big that you can't move it! But it's rolled away!

Imagine: a horrible, hopeless situation turned good. That's what the women found!

What did the man say to them?

He isn't _____, _____.

He's been _____.

God had done it! Jesus wasn't dead anymore.

How does that make you feel?

Sing your favourite praise song to God.

The women were told to tell the disciples about this amazing event. Who can you tell?

Jesus does it again!

Stretch your brain and see how many of Jesus' miracles you can remember in one minute. How many did you think of? Write the number here:

Read **John 21:1–6** to find out about another miracle Jesus did!

Jesus showed that he had power over fish, the sea, illness, blindness, bread, wine and even death. Tell Jesus how great his power is using all the BIGGEST words you know, or can make up. For example, "Your power is the tallest, powerfullest..."

Beach breakfast!

What is your favourite breakfast? Write your name and the menu here:

_____'s best breakfast

Read John 21:7–14.

Who was the cook?
What was he cooking?
How did he cook it?
Who did he cook it for?

Jesus knew his disciples would be hungry after a night out fishing, so he provided just what they needed – breakfast on the beach!

Jesus knows all about the things we need, too, and what is best for us. Be quiet and think about what you need the most. Now tell Jesus about it.

What next?

When you have finished your breakfast, what happens next? Perhaps you have to get ready for school, or put the food away. When Jesus and Peter finished their breakfast, they had a chat. Find out what they said.

Read John 21:15–17.

How many times did Jesus ask Peter if he loved him?

_____

How many times did Peter say he didn't know Jesus? (Look back to 6 April if you can't remember.)

_____

Jesus was showing Peter that he forgave him and he asked him to care for people, like a shepherd cares for his sheep.

Lord Jesus, thank you that, even though Peter made mistakes, you never stopped loving him. Thank you that you never stop loving me. Amen.

Forgiveness

Dave Godfrey tells this story.

When I was a boy I really liked helping my mum cook. An older boy at school named Scott, who I didn't know very well, knew I liked cooking. One day he lent me a brand new card, a bit like a top trumps card, which had a really cool cake recipe on it. But I didn't look after the card. It got mucky and torn. I tried to keep out of Scott's way. But I had this nagging feeling that God wanted me to knock on his front door, admit what I'd done and ask him to forgive me. In the end I asked God to help me. I went to his house and Scott was very happy to forgive me. I knew I had been brave and done the right thing. People usually forgive us if we are honest and really mean it when we say sorry.

Dave Godfrey takes RE lessons in schools, leads praise parties and children's clubs, trains children's workers and writes and sings some great wacky songs.

Hiding in caves

18 April

Do you like caves? Some caves are dark and smelly, but others are exciting and mysterious.

Read Judges 6:1–2, 7–10.

Did the Israelites like caves? Probably not! They were hiding from their enemies, the Midianites. Join the dots.

What did they ask God for? Fill in their speech bubble.

God had rescued them from their enemies before. He warned them that he was their God and they should worship him, but they didn't listen until they were in big trouble again. Then, at last, they asked God for help.

Thank God you can always call to him for help.

God can use anybody!

19 April

Are things going well for you today? If so – great! If not, perhaps you feel like Gideon. He was feeling scared, angry and weak.

Read Judges 6:11–16.

Write in the speech bubbles what the angel called Gideon (verse 12), and what words Gideon used to describe his family and himself (verse 15).

How did God encourage Gideon? Add the vowels:

Y _ _ c _ n d _ _ t b _ c _ _ s _
_ w _ l l h _ l p y _ _ .

Pray for the leaders of your country, school and church. Sometimes they're not as confident as they look!

Watch this!

Can you think of a story or film where the hero is in disguise? How do you know it's really them?

Read Judges 6:17–24.

Gideon wanted the visitor to prove that he was from God. What food did Gideon serve? Draw it here.

B_____

M_____

B_____

Draw fire burning up the food. (The fire was a sign that God accepted the offering.)
How did Gideon feel? Pleased? Bored? Terrified?
Write the name of Gideon's altar on the stones.

Lord, I praise you because you are so powerful.

chicken?

How brave are you?

Read Judges 6:25–31.

How brave was Gideon? Write the brave and cowardly things he did.

Brave	Cowardly

Everyone wanted to kill Gideon, but his father stood up for him. How brave was Joash!

To show your bravery, would you:

- sing a solo?
- pick up a spider or frog?
- own up and say sorry if you've done something wrong?
- tell someone you believe in Jesus?

Lord, help me to be brave enough to stand up for you.

Imagine the invisible

22 April

Which of these are powerful? Which can you see?

happiness   water   success

anger   space   rocket

Read Judges 6:33–35.

Unjumble four things missing from the picture and draw in three of them.

vriRe dJoanr _____

pmca _____

riiStp fo dGo _____

prttmeu _____

Which one can't you draw? Why?

Lord, I praise you for the power of your Spirit, even where I can't see him.

Yes? No? Not sure?

23 April

Have you ever wondered about dew? Why is the grass wet in the early morning, even when it hasn't rained?

Read Judges 6:36–40.

Gideon still wasn't convinced. Write **wet** and **dry** in the right place on each picture.

Tick the right boxes. Gideon's job was to:

☐ Thresh wheat.

☐ Make sheepskin jackets.

☐ Rescue Israel from the Midianites.

Gideon was worried that God might:

☐ Forget him.

☐ Be angry with him.

☐ Ignore him.

God's name

In Bible times, names usually had a meaning and people knew what the names meant.

God's people in Old Testament times used the Hebrew language. One name they used for God is Yahweh or Jehovah, but it was considered too holy to ever say or write in full. Its meaning is "I am who I am" or "I will be who I will be". This name was often put with another to make a long name describing something about God. Some of these names are:

JEHOVAH-JIREH: The Lord provides

JEHOVAH-ROPHE: The Lord your healer

JEHOVAH-SHALOM: The Lord is peace

EL ELYON: God Most High

EL: The creator

Even today some people don't like to say God's name and when they write it in English they put G_d.

Who's the best?

How many goals did your team last score? How much money have you got? Sometimes numbers are important.

Read Judges 7:1–3.

Write in the opposites to these words.

big
fat
difficult
afraid
stay
lose

Which ones are important in today's reading? Why?

Praise God because he is more powerful than the strongest government, the richest businessman, the fiercest army or the best football team.

God's victory

Read Judges 7:4–8.

Can you do sums?
You will find all the answers in your Bible.

☐ How many men were afraid and went back home? (**Judges 7:3**)

☐ How many men stayed with Gideon? (**Judges 7:3**)

☐ How many men was Gideon left with at the end? (**Judges 7:7**)

☐ Gideon started with (Answer 1 + Answer 2) men.

☐ The Lord told Gideon to send home (Answer 2 – Answer 3) men.

Can you find all the answers in the number square below? Cross them out and write the leftover numbers in order in the spaces below.

```
3 2 0 0 0
3 2 1 7 9
0 0 0 7 7
3 0 0 7 0
1 0 0 0 0
```

Even though Gideon lost
_ _, _ _ _ of his men, the Lord promised to give him the victory.
Judges _ : _

A special dream

Can you remember what you dreamed last night?

Read Judges 7:9–15.

Sometimes dreams are crazy! Draw a loaf of bread bigger than the tent!

This was a special dream, sent by God to encourage Gideon.
(Use Codebreaker 2 on page 48.)
What did the dream mean?

B2 C5 A4 / E3 B4 C2 C2 /
C2 A5 D5 / B2 B4 A4 A5 C5 C4 /
E3 B4 C4

_____

_____

What did Gideon do when he heard this?

E3 C5 D3 D4 B3 B4 D1 D1 A5 A4
/ B2 C5 A4

_____

_____

Lord, thank you for understanding me completely.

The winners!

How creative are you? Can you paint pictures, make things or invent stories? Are you full of ideas?

Read Judges 7:16–22.

Get two coloured pencils. With one colour, circle things you'd expect to need for a battle. With the other, circle the things Gideon used.

Find these words in the wordsearch: broke, shout, trumpet, torch, hundred, jar, three.

How were these words important in the story?

```
G O D S H O U T G
A V T R U M P E T
E V O I N C T B O
J A R R D Y T R O
G I C D R E O O N
S T H R E E S K M
A L L A D R M E Y
```

Make a sentence with the leftover letters:

_ _ _ / _ _ _ _ _ / _ _ _ _ _ _ _ /
_ _ / _ _ _ _ _ _ _ ' _ / _ _ _ _ _ /
_ _ _ _ .

Don't forget

Do you ever make the same mistake again and again?

Read Judges 8:22–27.

The people asked Gideon:

_____

Gideon replied:

_____

_____

But then he asked them for their gold earrings to make

_____

What was Gideon's big mistake? Look back to **Judges 6:25**. What did God tell him then?

_____ your father's altar to Baal.

_____ the symbol of the goddess Asherah/sacred pole.

(He should have known anyway, because one of the Ten Commandments is "Don't make idols".)

Lord, help me not to forget your instructions, or disobey them.

A sad ending

Have you ever read tombstones? Some have just a name and a date, but others have extra information like 'dear wife', or 'safe in the arms of Jesus'. What would you have written on Gideon's tombstone?

Read Judges 8:32–35.

Join the dots around Gideon's tombstone and write his name on it. Draw moss on it and weeds around it. People forgot Gideon and what he showed them about God.

Think of all the people who have told you about Jesus and helped you. Think of what they wanted you to remember. Thank God for them.

Love is everything

This week's Bible passage is often read at weddings. When Paul wrote this letter to the church in Corinth, in modern day Greece, he didn't know that people all around the world would still be reading it nearly 2,000 years later!

Read 1 Corinthians 13:1–3.

Not one of these five things is any good without love, but which of these is **not** mentioned in the Bible passage?

1 Speaking well, even in different languages.
2 Preaching amazing sermons.
3 Having faith to solve problems as big as mountains.
4 Being really generous.
5 Welcoming visitors into the church.

Lord God, money, brains and popularity are nothing if I don't have love in my heart. Help me to show your love in the way I live.

Love cares for others

2 May

Paul isn't just talking about huggy-kissy romantic love! He wants us to love like God loves, in everything we do. That's not easy!

Read 1 Corinthians 13:4–5.

We know that love is p _ _ _ _ _ _ _ and k _ _ _ (verse 4). But can you find seven things that love **is not** or that love **does not do** in this word square?

```
I L L A B C J D C
M A N N E R E D O
R E C O R D A U N
W R O N G S L O C
E F G H I J O R E
P O N H L K U P I
Q R S T U V S W T
I R R I T A B L E
S S E L F I S H D
```

(Answers are on page 192.)

Lord, when I feel like being grumpy, bad tempered and selfish, help me to show love instead.

Love perseveres

3 May

Sometimes the people we love are grumpy, cross or annoying. Sometimes they let us down. When that happens we have to work twice as hard at loving them. Do you think you ever make it hard for others to love you? Even a little?

Read 1 Corinthians 13:6–7.

Love is _____ with e _ _ _ (verse 6).

Love is _____ with the t _ _ _ _ _ (verse 6).

Can you name four great qualities that are part of love (verse 7)?

1 _____
2 _____
3 _____
4 _____

Father God, when I have disagreements with my friends and family, help me to go on loving them. Give us your love to help us work through our difficulties.

Love is everlasting

4 May

Have you ever had to take something back to a shop because it broke? Or perhaps someone has come to your house to fix your TV or washing machine? Nothing lasts for ever! Or does it?

Read 1 Corinthians 13:8–10.

What is the one thing that goes on for ever? Write it here in decorative writing.

And what three things does Paul say will not last for ever (verse 8)?

1 _____

2 _____

3 _____

Father God, thank you that your love is amazing. It goes on for ever and ever.

God loved us yesterday, he loves us today and he'll go on loving us tomorrow. His love is eternal.

Perfect vision

5 May

Have you ever looked at yourself in a spoon? Do you look better or worse than usual? In Bible times, mirrors were made out of polished metal, so they only gave a poor image.

Read 1 Corinthians 13:11–12.

Which sentence best explains the passage for you? 1 or 2?

1 Now we see life as in a dim mirror, but in heaven we will see things perfectly.

2 Now we see through the mist, but in heaven the sun will shine brightly.

Hold this page up to a mirror to discover the secret message.

One day we will see and understand everything just as clearly as God sees us.

Father God, as I grow up, help me to see you more clearly and help me to grow closer to you.

Love is most important

I love watching TV. I love ice cream sundaes. I love my family. Isn't it funny how the word love is used in different ways?

Read 1 Corinthians 13:13.

What three things will last for ever? Put one word in each circle, with the most important in the middle.

Write in this box something you've read about love this week.

Jesus was patient and kind. He was never jealous, conceited or proud; never rude, selfish or irritable.

He didn't keep a record of wrongs. Jesus never gave up on anyone and never let anyone down. Ask God to help you love like this.

Bullies beware!

Bullying is ALWAYS wrong. No one should make another person feel bad about who they are. Some reasons why kids bully might be:

- They get bullied themselves so they try and make themselves feel better by taking it out on others.
- They don't understand what other kids are like.
- They think it will make others think they're tough or cool.

How you deal with a bully can make a real difference. Here are some ideas.

1 Tell a teacher or your parents what's going on. They should listen to you and it's their job to help keep you safe.

2 Tell them to stop! A lot of bullies are cowards and will back down if you stand up for yourself.

3 Stay away from them if you can. Don't give them a chance to do the wrong thing.

4 Treat them really well. Defeat their badness with goodness. See what **Romans 12:21** says, and talk and pray with someone you trust about how to do it.

God's rules

8 May

How happy would school be if everyone kept the rules? Where does true happiness come from?

Read **Psalm 119:1–5** to find the answer.

These Bible words celebrate God's rules. God's Word (the Bible) is full of ideas to help us work out how to live the best life.

Make a poster with God's law (a book or scroll) in the middle. Across the top write: "Happy are those who live by God's Word." Around the edge draw five big speech bubbles. Each day this week look for something you didn't know before in God's Word. Write it in a speech bubble.

As you stick up the poster, sing praise to God for his Word.

How many verses has **Psalm 119** got? _____

(Psst! **Psalm 119** is the longest psalm! Which is the shortest? Keep checking. We'll tell you later.)

Learning to obey

9 May

How important is learning to obey rules? Imagine heavy vehicles and cars going the wrong way, jumping red lights, parking in the middle of the road! Chaos! This writer thinks obeying God's law is important.

Read **Psalm 119:9–16** and discover why!

To live a _____ life (verse 9).

To try to _____ God with all your heart (verse 10).

Not to _____ God (verse 11).

Why did the psalm writer read God's law? (Look at verses 14 and 16.) Why do you read the Bible? Think for a moment, then speak your answer out loud. (There's no wrong answer. You know why you do it.)

Tell God what you enjoy most about reading the Bible. Ask for help to obey God and live a pure life.

(Psst! Have you found the shortest psalm yet?)

Growing in confidence

Can you ride a bike? Do you remember what it was like before you could? Perhaps you needed someone to hold you, or extra wheels! But now you have confidence!

Read Psalm 119:49–52.

Some people are naturally confident. But the psalm writer's confidence does not come from being sure of himself, but from trusting in God's commands and promises.

Colour in the 'confidence-ometer'.

How confident are you...

...when kicking a football?

LOW					HIGH

...when playing an instrument?

LOW					HIGH

...when solving a puzzle?

LOW					HIGH

...when doing what is right?

LOW					HIGH

Thank you that I can always trust you. Amen.

Lasting for ever

Antiques are things which are very old – and often very valuable! Imagine finding something from the beginning of time and in perfect condition! It would be worth a fortune!

The psalm writer found something ancient that will last for ever! What is it?

Read Psalm 119:89–96.

Do you know what is the oldest thing in your house? It may be a clock, a toy, a picture or something else! How long has it been there? Will it last for ever? Probably not! Things get broken, and pictures fade!

Pick up your Bible. As you hold it, remember that God first spoke before the world was created. Say thank you to God for his Word.

(Psst! OK... the shortest Psalm is 117.)

Discovering wisdom

12 May

Who do you go to for advice? Maybe to a doctor, if you are ill. Or to a parent or friend, if you are in trouble. But what if you want advice on living the best life?

Read Psalm 119:97–105.

Wisdom is not about knowing facts for exams or having a good memory, but understanding how to live right.

Why do you think God's Word is like honey? Why is it like a light?

Read verse 97 again. Ask God to help you remember his laws all the time.

Next time you eat something sweet, ask God to give you wisdom.
Next time you're in the dark, ask God to show you the best way to live.

Is it possible to be wiser than all your teachers? Yes! But how? See verse 99.

Seeking justice

13 May

Do you ever think, "That's not fair!" when people get away with doing bad things? So did the psalm writer.

Read Psalm 119:137–144.

What does the writer say about God's law and character? Which verses have these words?

Fair/just

True/certain

God knows when things are unfair. God is also upset when people refuse to live right. God gave his law so that people would have guidelines for living fairly and sharing things. One day God will put all the wrong things right – for good!

Like the psalm writer, thank God for his promises (verse 140) and ask for wisdom to live right (verse 144).

Be a star – shine!

Being a Christian is about living for Jesus – loving him, obeying him and following him! It's like being a singer or an actor on stage with Jesus in the audience. We perform, or live, for him!

Jesus said, "Make your light shine, so that others will see the good that you do and will praise your Father in heaven" (**Matthew 5:16**). Jesus wants people shining for him!

How? Here's a few tips!

– Be careful about your words. Words can do a lot of good and a lot of damage!

– Always be kind and do what Jesus wants you to do – even if your friends are mean or start doing the wrong things.

– Be prepared. Think about what you would say if someone asked you why you are a Christian.

If you shine for Jesus then your friends will notice that you are a Christian, and they may want to become Christians, too!

Are you happy?

What makes you happy? Can you think of three things? In the next few days we will read what Jesus said about true happiness (or being blessed by God) and some of them sound very strange!

Ask God to help you understand what Jesus' words mean for you.

Read Matthew 5:1–4.

"Spiritually poor" means knowing how much we need God.

To "mourn" or "grieve" means to be really sad. How can you be happy if you're really sad?

Use Codebreaker 2 on page 48 to work out the message.

C1 C4 C5 E3 B4 C4 B2 /
B2 C5 A4/ B4 D4/ D5 D3 E1 A5 /
B3 A1 D1 D1 B4 C4 A5 D4 D4.

_____

_____

_____

Joy

Here's more of what Jesus said. Is this what most people believe about happiness?

Read Matthew 5:5–6.

Being humble and doing what God wants can sometimes be hard. So how do we remember to behave that way?

Jesus first

Others next

Yourself last

Can you spell out the word "joy" using your body?

Dear God, please help me to be humble and put other people before myself. Help me to put Jesus first and to do what you want. Amen.

Mercy

It's not always easy to be kind to other people, or put them first, but can you think of a time when someone did that for you? How did you feel?

Read Matthew 5:7.

True or false?

"Showing mercy", or "being merciful", is what God wants. **T/F**

Mercy is helping people in need. **T/F**

Mercy is forgiving someone else. **T/F**

Mercy is being kind and gentle towards other people. **T/F**

(Answers are on page 192.)

Remember these two words – joy and mercy. If we have one, it will help us to have the other!

Shut your eyes and think of someone you could be merciful to. Pray for that person now and ask God to help you.

pure

18 May

Imagine you are holding a bottle of spring water. It **looks** pure, but what does that mean? "Pure" means there is nothing wrong in it. ("Pure" is another important word to add to 'joy' and 'mercy'!)

Read Matthew 5:8.

Imagine this is you. With a pencil, write on the picture some of the things in your life that mean it isn't pure – the things that don't please God.

Tell God about them and ask him to forgive you and to make you pure. Use the eraser to rub out all those impure things!

When we say sorry for our sins, God doesn't rub it in – he rubs them out!

peacemaker

19 May

Be honest. Do you ever argue or fall out with your friends or brothers and sisters?

Who doesn't?! Look at the title to see another way to behave.

Read Matthew 5:9.

Imagine that you are at home with your family, or at school with your friends. Someone says something unkind to you. If you wanted to be a peace maker, what could you do? Write a peaceful answer in the speech bubble.

Please, God, help me to be a peace maker, not a peace breaker. Amen.

Tough times

Do you ever get laughed at or called names because you're a Christian? Jesus said we should expect it.

Read Matthew 5:10–12.

When people are mean to us because we follow Jesus it's no fun at all! But... these verses have a very important message. Use Codebreaker 2 on page 48 to find out what it is.

B2 C5 A4 / B4 D4 / C5 C4 / E5 C5 E1 D3 / D4 B4 A4 A5.

_____

_____

_____

Please, God, help me to understand your way to be truly happy or blessed. Please help me when it's difficult. If other people give me a hard time, help me to remember that you are with me. Amen.

Salty

Do you like your chips plain or with plenty of salt and vinegar? What about you, are you salty?

Read Matthew 5:13.

We use salt to make the flavours of our food stand out. How can you be like salt to all the people you meet? Fill in the missing vowels:

By being:
m _ r c _ f _ l
p _ r _
p _ _ c _ m _ k _ r s
h _ m b l _
_ b _ d _ _ n t

Where have you seen those words before?

Imagine shaking salt onto your tea. How far do all the little grains travel? Now think of all the people you know. Ask God to help your "salt" to reach them.

Did you know: at times, Roman soldiers were paid in salt instead of coins!

Floodlights!

22 May

Have you ever seen a floodlit building or sports field? It shows up really clearly in the dark.

Read Matthew 5:14–16.

Imagine switching on a torch and then putting it in a cupboard! What would be the point of that? Instead, you use it to give out light.

Write your answers in yellow or orange:

Who should see your light?

What will they see?

Who will be praised?

Read these words carefully and only pray them if you really mean them:

Dear God, please help me to be obedient to you so that I shine out for others. I want people to learn more about you when they see me.

Pentecost

23 May

Pentecost is sometimes called "the birthday of the church". See if you can work out why:

When Jesus went back into heaven after rising from the dead he told his friends to stay in Jerusalem and wait for the Holy Spirit.

A few days later, during the Jewish festival of Pentecost, the Holy Spirit came. Jesus' friends were meeting together when they heard a sound like a roaring wind and saw what looked like flames on their heads. The Holy Spirit filled them and gave them special gifts to help them tell others about Jesus. Many hundreds of people became believers that day and the church began to spread around the world.

You can read about the Day of Pentecost in **Acts 2**. If you read the rest of Acts you'll find out how the church grew.

Challenge: see if you can find out how old your church is.

Dear Dave

24 May

My friends have started to say some nasty things to me because I am a Christian. What should I do? Tom.

Dear Tom,

Sometimes being a Christian is not easy. People tend to pick on others when they are different from them. Christians are different because we live for Jesus and do what he says. Sometimes our friends don't understand and can say some hurtful things! Here's a few things you can do!

1 Pray for your friends and ask God to help them understand your faith.

2 Remember, Jesus said: "God blesses those people who are treated badly for doing right" (**Matthew 5:10–11**).

3 Be patient – often these things last only a short while.

4 Be good – don't retaliate, but keep caring for your friends.

5 Talk to someone you trust about it and ask them to pray for you and your friends.

6 Forgive your friends!

Dave

Promises

25 May

Do you make promises? Do you keep your promises? God made lots of promises about Jesus hundreds of years before he was born. God kept his promises. Meet Isaiah. He was God's messenger and it was his job to tell people what God promised.

Read Isaiah 51:1–3.

These verses are hard to understand, but Isaiah was reminding everyone about promises that God had made, and kept!

Meet Abraham.

Draw what God promised and then gave him. (Check out **Genesis 15:5**.)

Thank you, God, that we can rely on all your promises in the Bible.

Light

26 May

We often take light for granted — until it's dark, then we realise how important it is!

The message that God gave Isaiah was about light...

Read Isaiah 51:4–5.

What did God say that his people should do?

Circle the right picture:

What did God say that his laws would bring to the people? (Cross out the wrong ones.)

money   good luck   light

Dear God, please help me to listen to your laws and messages in the Bible. Thank you that they are like light and show me the right way to live. Amen.

(Psst! When Jesus came, he said something special about light. Check out **John 8:12** to find out what it was.)

Have a look!

27 May

If possible, go outside and look at the sky. If not, look out of a window. What can you see?

Draw or write it here:

Read Isaiah 51:6–8.

Can you work out what the verses are saying?

1 day the will end but

God has a to save

 4ever

All of us who belong to Jesus will be safe with him no matter what happens.

Thank God that he loves us so much that he made a plan to rescue us.

In the beginning

28 May

What things make you feel scared or unsafe?
Imagine God chasing those things away.

Read Isaiah 51:12–16.

Which verses tell us that God created the world?
Verses _____ and _____.

They remind us that God is very
tearg _ _ _ _ _ and
fowpuler _ _ _ _ _ _ _ _.
(Unjumble the words.)

God promises to keep his people strong/encouraged (verse 12) and safe (verse 16).That's awesome!

(Psst! In these verses, "strong" means having God's help to make you strong in your spirit, not in your muscles!)

Ask God to help you to be strong when you feel weak.

Write in very tiny writing somewhere: "God will keep me strong and safe."

Good news, bad news

29 May

Just sometimes, God lets disasters happen so that his people will stop doing bad things and turn back to him.

Read Isaiah 51:17–23.

Jerusalem, wake up! Stand up! You've drunk too much from the cup filled with the Lord's anger. You have swallowed every drop, and you can't walk straight. Not one of your many children is there to guide you or to offer a helping hand. You have been destroyed by war and by famine; I cannot comfort you. The Lord your God is angry, and on every street corner your children lie helpless, like deer trapped in nets. You are in trouble and drunk, but not from wine. So pay close attention to the Lord your God, who defends you and says, "I have taken from your hands the cup filled with my anger that made you drunk. You will never be forced to drink it again. Instead I will give it to your brutal enemies, who treated you like dirt and walked all over you."

Underline all the bad things that God had allowed to happen. Draw a happy face next to the good news for the people of Jerusalem.

Your God is king!

It's great to get some good news, especially when things haven't been going well. Jerusalem was at war, but look what happened.

Read Isaiah 52:7–12.

Read verse 7 again, then fill in the missing vowels:

What was the good news?

P _ _ c _ !

What did the messenger announce?

Y_ _ r G_d _s K_ ng!

When God rules, there is peace. When we turn away from our sins and turn to God, God rules as King of our lives.

Thank you, God, that you love us and want to be King of our lives. Amen.

Guess who?

Try this with your family or a friend. Describe someone they know, or a famous person. How long before they guess who you are talking about?

Read Isaiah 52:13–15.

Who could these verses be describing?

Read them to someone else and see what they think. Here are some more clues:

His father on earth was called Joseph. He was born about 2,000 years ago. Until he was 30 he worked as a carpenter. He trained 12 men to spread his message. Write his name in the thought bubble:

Thank you, God, for sending your Son to earth as your servant, to rescue us from our sins. Amen.

Quick quiz

1 June

How much attention have you been paying during this Snapshots? Join the questions/statements to their answers.

What did Jesus give his friends on the beach?

Where Joseph came from.

Who denied he knew Jesus?

What never fails?

Who asked God to make a sheep's fleece wet or dry?

Jesus said, "You are like....."

Gideon

Breakfast

Salt

Arimathea

Peter

Love

The servant

2 June

Do you ever wish you had a servant? What would you make your servant do for you? This Bible bit calls Jesus a servant.

Read Isaiah 53:1–3 for a description of God's servant. Which of these sums up what you have read?

- [ ] He had nothing that would make us notice him.
- [ ] He was someone who stood out in a crowd.
- [ ] Jesus did everything God wanted him to do.
- [ ] He was God's servant.
- [ ] He came to serve us, too. He even gave his life for us.

Write or draw about how that makes you feel. Look at what you have written or drawn and talk to God about it.

Instead of me

3 June

Did you ever do something wrong, but others thought someone else did it so you didn't get into trouble?

Read Isaiah 53:4–6.

Put the words from the sheep in the right

Jesus cross never wrong we punished us

When _____ died on the _____ he had _____ done anything _____. He was being _____ instead of _____, for the things _____ do wrong.

Read verse 6 again (aloud if you can), and instead of the words "we" or "all of us" at the end of the verse, say your name instead. Then talk to God about what you have said.

I don't deserve it!

4 June

Remember what we read about God's anger? Look back to 29 May.

Read Isaiah 53:7–9 to find out what Jesus did so God wouldn't be angry with us.

Jesus didn't **have** to suffer, but he chose to. Why do you think he did that?

Check out **Romans 5:8** to help you think about your answer.

Read the verses again. Stop at the end of each verse and think quietly about it. Tell God what you think about these things. Then read the next verse.

Dear God, help me never to forget what Jesus did for me.

Forgiven!

Do you find it easy to forgive someone when they have hurt your feelings or done something wrong that affects you? Be honest!

Find out what God does for us because Jesus died on the cross.

Read Isaiah 53:10–12.

Because Jesus was punished instead of us, God forgives us. Just like that. That's **so** amazing!

Do you remember Jesus' words about forgiveness when he was dying? Read **Luke 23:34** and write them here.

_____

_____

_____

_____

Thank God for forgiving you and ask him to help you to forgive others.

Amazing words!

Sometimes, when very small children are cross, they say: "I don't love you anymore!" But God never does.

Read Isaiah 54:6–10.

☐ How many times does the word "love" or "loves" appear in these few verses?

☐ How many times can you find God promising something?

These verses are about how much God loves us, even though we don't deserve it. He forgives us and he never stops loving us! Awesome!

On a big piece of paper draw a mountain. Write the words of verse 10 around your poster. Stick it up as a reminder of how much God loves you.

Thank God for his love for you as you draw.

It's a date!

7 June

Have you ever wondered how we got our calendar?

The history of our world is divided into two sections. The first section is called BC, which stands for "Before Christ". This is the time before Jesus Christ was born. The dates in this era get bigger the further back in time you go.

The second section is called CE which stands for Common or Christian Era. (It is also called AD which stands for Anno Domini, which is Latin for "in the year of our Lord".) This is the time in which we are living now, after Jesus was born.

From year one, which is the date of the birth of Jesus, calendar dates are calculated forwards for the era. So our calendar is based around the life of Jesus.

How cool is that!

What a boatful!

8 June

What would you say if a famous person asked to borrow your bike or scooter?

Simon got an unexpected reward when he lent something to Jesus.

Read Luke 5:1–7.

So many people wanted to hear Jesus that he ended up teaching from a very unusual place!
Draw it here.

After he'd finished teaching, what did Jesus tell Simon to do with the boat?

What did Simon reply?

Draw what happened on your picture.

Look again at verse 5 and then pray:

Dear Jesus, help me to trust you like Simon did.

catch!

What would you say to someone who did something amazing to help you?

Read Luke 5:8–11.

What did Simon say when he saw his boat full of fish? (Tick the right box.)

☐ Thank you.

☐ Don't come near me! I'm sinful!

☐ Wow! That's brilliant.

What did Jesus reply? (Tick the right box.)

☐ Yes, you are sinful.

☐ That's OK.

☐ Don't be afraid. From now on you'll catch people.

(Psst! Jesus was giving these fishermen the job of telling others about him.)

Read verse 11 again. Now make a list of your favourite toys, games and sports gear. Walk away from it and talk with Jesus about whether he's more important to you than these things.

who to choose?

How do you pick teams for games at school? Jesus picked really unexpected people to be in his team.

Read Luke 5:27–32.

Who did Jesus pick at the tax office?

Sam   Ben   Levi   Tom

Many people hated tax collectors because they worked for the Romans and often cheated people. So people were shocked that Jesus spent time with them.

Cross out the wrong answers in Jesus' message.

"Who needs a doctor? The well/ the sick.

I came to call sinners/good people to turn back to God."

Thank you, God, that you don't expect us to be perfect before you invite us to follow you.

Tax fact: in many countries, taxes are collected from people to help pay for schools, hospitals and lots of other things!

Choosing

What do you do when you have an important choice to make? What did Jesus do?

Read **Luke 6:12–16** about Jesus choosing people for his special mission.

Jesus needed God's help to choose the right people. He needed somewhere quiet so he could concentrate on praying. Where did he go?
How long did he spend praying?

How many of the 12 names do you recognise? Can you remember what they did? (Matthew was probably another name for Levi.)
No joke! What's the difference between an apostle and a disciple?

Disciple = someone who learns from a teacher

Apostle = someone sent out with a message

Jesus wants you to follow him, too. What will you say?
Talk with Jesus about what he may want you to be and do for him.

"Jesus is coming!"

Imagine you are in a big crowd waiting for something exciting to happen. That's what it was like in today's reading.

Read Luke 6:17–19.

Large crowds had come to see Jesus. Find three places they had come from:

1 _____
2 _____
3 _____

What had the people come for? (Fill in the missing vowels.)

T_ h_ _r J_s_s t_ _ch.

T_ b_ h_ _l_d.

T_ t_ _ ch J_s_s.

What happened when the people came to Jesus?

P_w_r w_nt fr_m h_m _nd h_ h_ _l_d th_m _ll.

Imagine that Jesus has come to your town or village. What do you want him to do for you? Tell him. And listen hard to what he might say to you.

Gatecrasher!

Think about the last time someone came to your house for a meal.
What did you eat? How did you prepare?

Simon the Pharisee would have wanted everything to go well when Jesus came for dinner...

Read Luke 7:36–43.

What happened in the middle of dinner? (Number the sentences in order.)

A woman:

- [ ] dried Jesus' feet with her hair.
- [ ] stood by Jesus, crying.
- [ ] poured perfume on Jesus' feet.
- [ ] wet his feet with her tears.
- [1] came in with a jar of perfume.
- [ ] kissed Jesus' feet.

Read verse 39 again. Do you think Jesus knew what she was like? Do you think he minded her coming to him?

Thank you, Jesus, that you never turn anyone away.

Who is this?

Simon was shocked when the woman gate-crashed his party, but he was even more astounded by what Jesus said to her.

Read Luke 7:44–50.

What did Jesus tell the woman (verse 48)? Write it in the speech bubble.

Then what did Jesus say to her (verse 50)?

How do you think the woman felt when she went home?

Now wash your hands (use liquid soap if you've got some). As you rub the soap in, say sorry for any wrong things you've done. As you rinse the soap off, remember that Jesus has "washed away" your sins and forgiven you. How do you feel?

Wordsearch

Find the names of the 12 men Jesus chose in the wordsearch. Can you do it without checking back to see who they all were? If you need help, look at **Luke 6:14–16**.

```
S A M B S A L E X
T I M A N D R E W
U D V R C R A I G
P U G T H O M A S
J H S H R E A G I
S J I O J S T A M
A U M L D O T R O
D D O O I J H Y N
U E N M Y P E N E
J A M E S X W F O
B O R W S E M A J
```

(Psst! Two names appear twice.)

God is powerful

The most powerful people in the world are nowhere near as powerful as our great God.

Read Psalm 105:1–6.

Can you find eight different instructions in these verses that tell us what to do? The last is "Remember his miracles", but what comes before that? Write them in this octagon.

Let's do as the psalmist suggests.

Thank God for the good things in your life (verse 1).

Praise God for something (verse 2).

Trust God when you need help (verse 4).

Remember one of God's miracles and then **praise God** because he is powerful (verse 5).

God keeps his promises

How long could you keep each of these promises?

I promise to keep my room tidy.

I promise not to eat chocolate or crisps.

I promise never to tell a lie.

Read Psalm 105:7–11.

God made promises (or covenants) to Abraham, Isaac and Jacob. (Can you remember what any of them were? Check out **Genesis 12:1–3** or **28:15**.)

But the promises weren't just for Abraham and his family.

How long will God's promises last?

- [ ] 100 years.
- [ ] 1,000 years.
- [ ] thousands of years.

So God's promises last for ever! That means they're for you and me, too!

Thank you, God, for keeping your promises.

God's special plan

Have you ever tried to complete a difficult jigsaw puzzle without looking at the picture on the box? It's really hard. Sometimes life seems really puzzling, but we don't need to worry because God knows what the big picture looks like.

Read Psalm 105:12–22.

What sad thing happens to the people (verse 16)? In verses 17 and 18 Joseph is a slave in chains in Egypt, but where does he finish up? God was in control of what was happening.

Think about some of the sad situations in the world at the moment.

God can see the big picture. Ask him to be in control.

Did you know? Abraham, Jacob and Joseph lived nearly 2,000 years before Jesus was born.

God of creation

Can you remember something important that happened last year? What about something important you've learnt about in history?

The psalmist was encouraging people to remember what God had done for his people.

Read Psalm 105:26–33.

God created our world and everything in it, and he has complete power over his creation. He can make it do whatever he wants.

Draw lines to connect each verse with the part of creation that it mentions.

28	Insects
29	Weather
30	Fruit, plants and trees
31	Water, rivers and fish
32	Light and dark
33	Frogs and all animals

Think of something God has done for you or your family. Can you write a poem or psalm about it? Use it to praise God.

God provides

Draw a circle around anything that you would take with you on a day trip to a place you had not visited before.

**money   drink   packed lunch
plant pot   potato peeler   map**

Some of the things were ridiculous – but you knew just what you'd need! In the same way, God knows what his people need.

Read Psalm 105:37–42.

Cross out the wrong pictures.
What God gave the Israelites to eat...

...and to drink

What they used for money.

How God lit up their path.

A happy ending

21 June

God helped Moses and the Israelites to escape from slavery in Egypt. He led them through the desert for many years and finally he brought them to the new land that he had promised them. Read what happened next.

Read Psalm 105:43–45.

Think about how life changed for the Israelites...

THEN

They were slaves.

They were sad.

They had no home.

NOW

They are free.

So they_____

God gives them a new_____

So they_____

Fill in the vowels:

P r _ _ s _ t h _ L _ r d !

Think back over your life. What sad things have happened? What good things have happened? God has been there all the time. What do you want to say to him?

Bible club

22 June

Have you ever been to a holiday Bible club? See if what you did is anything like what they do in Romania...

Romania is a large country in Eastern Europe that has beautiful mountains, deep forests where wild bears live and a small coastline on the Black Sea.

Have you ever been so cold that putting on more clothes makes no difference? Children living in the countryside can feel like that in winter when the temperature can drop to -25°C!

In summer, the temperature can soar to 45°C. That's when Scripture Union runs holiday Bible clubs so that children can learn about Jesus, have lots of fun and make new friends.

Prayer page

Dave Godfrey says:

One of my friends once taught me to pray 'Teaspoon' prayers! Teaspoon prayers are TSP prayers – Thank you, Sorry, Please. It's very simple, but it is very powerful. When Jesus taught his disciples to pray, he told them to:

T: Thank God for who he is and for what he has done.

S: Say sorry for the bad things we have done and forgive people who have done things wrong to us.

P: Ask him to provide for all we need and to protect us from the devil. Jesus said that we should also ask God for his will to be done.

So there you have it. Next time you sit down at the table to eat and you are holding a teaspoon, remember to pray, because God loves it!

PS Look up **Matthew 6:9–13** and see if you can find the TSP bits.

Fight for God

Does the Bible tell us to fight? Yes! Christians are told to fight the devil, who is our enemy. Don't worry – we have God's power on our side!

Read Ephesians 6:10–13.

God gives Christians the "armour" that they need to protect them from evil, just like a Roman soldier's armour. Fill in the gaps with 'e' or 'o'.

H_lm_t_

Br_astplat_

Shi_ld

B_lt

Sw_rd

Sh_ _s

Read verse 10 again, then thank God that he is so strong and he helps us to be strong with him as we fight against evil.

Truth and righteousness

25 June

Look at the picture of the Roman soldier on page 94. Today's verse is about a belt and a breastplate/armour.

Read Ephesians 6:14.

If you can, find a belt and tie it around your middle, then tuck a sheet of A4 paper into it at the front, like a breastplate!

So that we are always ready in our fight against evil, we need to make sure that we have the truth about Jesus wrapped around us, like a **belt**.

"Righteousness" or "justice" means living God's way. If we do right, it will protect us just like a **breastplate** protected a Roman soldier.

Thank you, God, that the truth about Jesus and living your way protects us from the devil. Amen.

Be ready!

26 June

If you haven't got any shoes on, can you put some on now? No soldier goes to battle in bare feet! That's what today's verse is about – being ready!

Are you ready to obey these commands?

Attention! (Stand ready.)

Quick march!

Halt! (Stop.)

About turn!

At ease! (Relax.)

Read Ephesians 6:15.

What should we always be ready to do in our fight against evil?
- [ ] Wait until tomorrow.
- [ ] Talk about war.
- [ ] Share God's peace.
- [ ] Show other people that we love Jesus.

Take off your shoes and hold them while you pray. Ask God to help you to be ready to share his peace.

Codebreaker 3

A	B	C	D	E	F	G	H	I	J
26	25	24	23	22	21	20	19	18	17

K	L	M	N	O	P	Q	R	S	T
16	15	14	13	12	11	10	9	8	7

U	V	W	X	Y	Z
6	5	4	3	2	1

Codebreaker 4

	1	2	3	4	5
	A	B	C	D	E
	F	G	H	I	J
	K	L	M	N	O
	P	Q	R	S	T
	U	V	W	X	Y

Protection

Ask someone in your family to make some paper darts and throw them at you. Use a large book, or a tray to fend them off. How did you get on?

Read Ephesians 6:16.

The Bible tells us that trust in Jesus is like a shield to protect us. Read this rhyme.

Can you say it without looking?

> Trust in Jesus to help you to be strong, when you are tempted to do something wrong.

Are you struggling to do the right thing at school, or with your friends? Pray about it now!

Lord God, please help me to hold faith like a shield.

Did you know that faith isn't something we make up ourselves? It's a gift from God! Check out **Ephesians 2:8–9**.

The fish is fitting

Some Christians wear a badge shaped like a fish or drive a car with a fish sticker on the back. Do you know why? When the church began it was dangerous to be a Christian. People who followed Jesus were often killed, so they needed a secret sign to help them recognise each other without others knowing. Christians chose the fish. It was a good idea because seven of Jesus' disciples were fishermen and Jesus said that one day they would catch "people instead of fish" (**Luke 5:10**). But it was cleverer than that! The Greek word for fish is "ichthus". If you take each letter of that word in Greek you can make an important message.

Iesous (Jesus)

CHristos (Christ)

THeou (God's)

Uios (Son)

Soter (Saviour)

Next time you're in church, see how many fish you can spot.

Your sword

Pick up your Bible and hold it out in front of you. Did you know that you are holding a sword? Well, you are!

Read Ephesians 6:17.

 is like

Why? Cross out the wrong answer:

1 It makes us feel important

or

2 It is like a weapon that God has given us to fight against evil.

It's no good having the Bible as a weapon against evil if we don't read it!

Ask God to help you to read your Bible. Pray that all the other Snapshots readers around the world will build up their strength in God as they read.

Get reading, sword-wielders! The Bible prepares us for life!

Pray!

Do people ever tell you the same thing several times, just to make sure you've got the message? It happens in today's Bible verse...

> Never stop praying, especially for others. Always pray by the power of the Spirit. Stay alert and keep praying for God's people.

Ephesians 6:18

Use a pen to:

Underline the first three words in the first sentence.

Underline the first two words in the middle sentence.

Underline the fourth and fifth words in the final sentence.

Get the message?

Dear God, please help me to (say the words you underlined). I pray for _____. Amen.

Cut out a 'P' shape to carry as a secret reminder to pray.

Long ago

Imagine you are somewhere really dark. You can't see anything – and it's hard to believe there's anything out there at all. Long, long, long ago there wasn't!

Read Genesis 1:1–5.

Before the earth even existed, who was there? To find out, colour in the shapes that contain a dot.

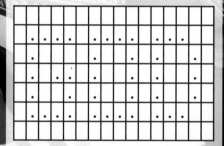

God has always been here. There's never been a time when God didn't exist.
God didn't want to leave every-thing dark and shapeless. What did he create on the first day?

D _ _ and N _ _ _ _

So God has always been here. Tell God how that makes you feel.

Just say the word

Imagine making something just by telling it to be made! It's not possible... or is it?

Read Genesis 1:6–8.

Use Codebreaker 3 on page 96 to find out how God made things.

20 12 23 / 24 12 14 14 26 13 23 22 23 / 26 13 23 / 18 7 / 4 26 8 / 23 12 13 22

_____

_____

_____

God is so powerful that he only had to speak and things were made.
What did God create on the second day?

_ _ _

Look at the sky (remember not to look at the sun!). How would you describe it to someone from another planet?

Thank God for making the sky.

On the third day...

Think about the last meal you had. How much of what you ate had grown in a field, orchard or garden?

Read Genesis 1:9–13

Unscramble the words below to find out what God created on the third day.

terah _____

esa _____

lla nidks fo santpl

_____

When God created plants he didn't just make things that would grow once and die. He also made plants that would keep on producing year after year.

Thank you, God, for making crops and vegetables and fruit. My favourite fruit is _____. I like _____ as well. Thank you for making food that is good for me and tastes yummy as well.

Lord of everything

When do you get up? When do you go to bed? What's your favourite season of the year?

All these questions have one thing in common.

Read Genesis 1:14–19.

In the space below, draw what God created on the fourth day.

When God created day and night, seasons and festivals, he was making something he knew we needed. Use a mirror to find out what: **EMIT**

Imagine what life would be like without time! It would be chaos! Dear God, some times are annoying, like _____ _____. Some times are great, like _____ _____.

Time can seem to go too fast or too slowly... but we cannot do without it. Thank you for time.

Living creatures

5 July

God had created a wonderful world, but there was nothing to enjoy it.

Read Genesis 1:20–23.

How many different birds can you name in one minute?

Now try it with sea creatures.

Even if you thought of lots, God has created loads more. God has made a fantastic assortment of creatures.

Use the letters below to write a prayer about God's creatures. The first two lines are there to help you get started.

For all your amazing creatures
I thank you, Lord

S _____

H _____

B _____

I _____

R _____

D _____

S _____

And finally...

6 July

Find a book about birds or animals to discover some you've never heard of.

Read Genesis 1:24–31.

Fill in the missing vowels (a, e, i, or o) to see what God created on the sixth day.

_ n _ m _ ls

_ n d   p _ _ p l _

How do you feel when you've finished a piece of work?

What did God think of all that he had made? (Look at verse 31.)

There's nothing wrong with feeling pleased when we have done well or worked hard on something.

God provided enough food for everyone to eat (verses 29–30). Sadly, we have spoiled God's world and some people no longer have enough to eat.

Pray for people who are starving or struggling to find enough food.

Finished!

7 July

Have you ever done something really hard? What did you feel like afterwards?

Read Genesis 2:1–4.

What day was it when God had finished his work?

What did God do when he had finished?

God blessed the seventh day and made it special.

What do you do on the seventh day (Sunday) to keep it special?

Thank you, God, that when you created the world you made space for both work and rest. Help me to work hard when I am _____

_____

_____.

Thank you that I can rest when

_____

_____.

Amen.

Man!

8 July

Have you ever made a clay model? If you don't like it or if it goes wrong you can squash it up and start again.

Read Genesis 2:4–7.

Cross out all the Xs and Zs to find the answers to the questions.

What did God make man out of?

SXOZIXL FZRXOZM TXHZE GXRZOXUZNXD

What did God put into man?

LXIZFXE-ZGXIZVXIZNXG BXRZEXAZTXH

How did God decide what man would be like?

Look back to **Genesis 1:26–27**.

God knew exactly how he was going to make a man. He didn't need to experiment first. God planned everything carefully.

Tell God how it feels to know that he planned you and gave you life.

We're here to care

9 July

If you were given a beautiful present, what would you do with it?

Read Genesis 2:8–9,15.

God put man in a beautiful garden.

Find two things the man was there to do.

1 _____

2 _____

Right from the start God made man responsible for looking after the world.

Can you think of ways that we are no longer caring for the world properly? (You can look in a newspaper for ideas.)

Are there any things you can do to help put things right? (Have you thought of recycling things? Are you careful not to drop litter?)

Thank you, God, for your beautiful world. I am sorry for the ways in which everyone has spoiled it. Help us to care for it better now and in the future.

Rules!

10 July

Can you think of any rules you have at school or at home?

When God made people he gave them clear rules.

Read Genesis 2:15–17.

What did God say people could and could not do?

Fill in the table below:

You may	You must not

When God said people would die if they disobeyed him, it meant they would lose the opportunity to live for ever.

God made rules for good reasons, to help us live together. Try to imagine what people and the world would be like without them.

Dear God, sometimes I find rules annoying, but I understand that we need them. Please help me to keep school rules – and to live every day by your rules.

company

11 July

Imagine being alone on an island for a week. How would you feel?

Read Genesis 2:18–24.

Are these statements true or false?

God didn't care that the man was alone. **T/F**

God decided to make a companion for the man. **T/F**

The man named the animals and birds. **T/F**

The animals were equal friends with the man. **T/F**

God made a woman out of soil. **T/F**

The man was very pleased with the woman. **T/F**

(Answers on page 192.)

Thank you, God, that you give us what we need. Thank you for all my family and friends, especially

_____.

Is there anyone at school who is lonely? What can you do to help them? To begin with, you can ask God to be with them.

Just like God

12 July

In what different ways could you tell your friends a message? What does God do?

Read Hebrews 1:1–3.

First God used prophets to tell his message, then he sent his Son. Put the words in their right place.

heaven	exactly
God	glory
Forgives	Sits
created	brightness

Jesus:

Is the one through whom God _ _ _ _ _ _ _ the universe.

Reflects the _ _ _ _ _ _ _ _ _ _ of God's _ _ _ _ _.

Is _ _ _ _ _ _ _ like _ _ _.

_ _ _ _ _ _ _ _ _ our sins.

_ _ _ _ next to God in _ _ _ _ _ _.

Try to imagine Jesus in glory and power. What would you say to him?

The greatest of all time!

13 July

What would you say about the greatest person you know?

Here's how great Jesus is.

Read Hebrews 1:4–8.

Angels are important but Jesus is God's Son. That's much greater!

What did God say the angels should do (verse 6)?

Write the answer in the speech bubble.

Sing your favourite worship song to Jesus.

Remember, angels are God's messengers and are not cute with tinsel hair!

What's Jesus like?

14 July

How would you describe one of your friends to someone who didn't know them? Would you say what they look like or what sort of person they are?

If anyone asked you what Jesus was like, what would you say?

Read Hebrews 1:9–12.

Cross out the Xs and Zs to describe Jesus:

LXOZVXEZS RXIZGXHZT AXNZD
HXAZTXEZS WXRZOXNZG
CXHZOXSZEXN BZY GXOZD
AXLZWXAZYXS TZHXE SZAXMZE
LXIZVXEZS FXOZR EXVZEXR

What new things have you learned about Jesus this week? Talk with God about your discoveries.
Ask him to help you to keep learning more.

Make a poster that describes Jesus. Ask if you can put it up in your church.

Winners

Imagine that your favourite sports star has just won a championship. What would the award ceremony be like?

Jesus was crowned with glory and honour. Why?

Read Hebrews 2:9–10.

Use Codebreaker 3 on page 96 to find out why Jesus is a winner.

17 22 8 6 8 /
23 18 22 23 /
7 12 / 8 26 5 22 /
/ 6 8

_ _ _ _ _ /
_ _ _ _ /
_ _ /
_ _ _ _ /_ _

If Jesus hadn't died, we wouldn't be forgiven by God.

Now use the code to find out how Jesus makes us winners.

4 22 / 8 19 26 9 22 / 19 18 8 / 20 15 12 9 2

_ _ / _ _ _ _ _ / _ _ _ /
_ _ _ _ _

Because Jesus died, we can live with God for ever!

God says Jesus is a winner for dying for us. What would you give Jesus a medal for? Turn your ideas into a prayer.

Hard questions

Can you answer these tough questions?

What has Jesus' death got to do with the devil?

Why is it good for us that Jesus suffered and was tempted?

Look for the answers as you read.

Read Hebrews 2:14–18.

Jesus didn't just stay in heaven and feel sorry for us. He did something about it – he became like us so he could save us.

Read verse 18 again. We are tempted when we feel like doing something bad or when we don't feel like doing something we should. What are you tempted to do, or not do? Talk to God about it. He's been there, he understands.

Jesus was tempted but he never did anything wrong.

Jesus in charge

17 July

What's your house like? Draw it on a piece of paper.

Read Hebrews 3:1–6.

The writer to the Hebrews describes God's people as being like a house. Who built the house (verse 4)?

Write his name under the house.

Who's in charge of the house (verse 6)? Write the name in the roof.

Inside the house, write the names of any people you know who love and serve God. (Don't forget yourself!)

Thank you, Jesus, that you are in charge of your people. Please help (read out the list of names in your house picture) to keep hoping in you.

An ancient prayer

18 July

Most of us talk with God using the same sorts of words we'd use to talk with our friends. But people have been praying through the centuries and sometimes it's good to use prayers that other Christians have used. Here's one that was first prayed by Richard of Chichester who lived from 1197 to 1253, when the English language was rather different from how it is now.

Do you think you could memorise this prayer? Is there someone in your church or family that you could challenge to learn it, too?

Perhaps you could make it a family prayer and use 'we' instead of 'I'.

Day by day, dear Lord,
of thee three things I pray:
To see thee more clearly,
Love thee more dearly,
Follow thee more nearly,
Day by day.

The story begins...

Everyone in New York remembers 9/11, when the Twin Towers were destroyed in 2001.

Everyone in Jerusalem remembered 597 BC, when the Babylonians invaded and the city walls were destroyed.

Read Nehemiah 1:1–4.

Nehemiah had been taken as a prisoner from Jerusalem to Babylon, and he'd done well there. He was an important royal servant. But he missed Jerusalem.

Tick what sort of book you think Nehemiah's book is:

☐ Adventure ☐ Spy story
☐ History ☐ Geography
☐ Soap ☐ Hero's success

Did you tick them all?

Nehemiah didn't do what we expect heroes to do. What three things did he do?
Unjumble the letters to find out:

e t p w _____

n u o m r d e _____

d y p e a r _____

Prayer like a diamond

Have you seen a real diamond? It has lots of sides, and it reflects lots of colours if you turn it around.

Read Nehemiah 1:5–11.

Prayer has lots of sides like a diamond: praise, thanks, saying sorry, remembering God's promises, trusting him, asking.

Label the parts of Nehemiah's prayer in this diamond and colour each part a different colour.

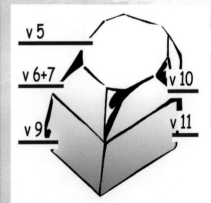

Nehemiah talked to God about everything that was important to him and his friends. Do you talk to God about everything?

God gives courage

21 July

In Alice in Wonderland, Alice was afraid to get anything wrong in case the queen said, "Off with her head!"

Read Nehemiah 2:1–4.

How long had Nehemiah prayed about Jerusalem? (Clue: Check out **Nehemiah 1:4**.) Have you ever prayed about anything for that long?

It was time to ask special permission from the emperor. What if the emperor was furious? Nehemiah needed to be very brave.

Draw Jerusalem's broken walls in one thought bubble, and what he feared from the emperor in the other.

Ask God to make you brave.

A big YES!

22 July

Horse riding, designing, building, making things, leading a team – what are you good at? Nehemiah had to do them all!

Read Nehemiah 2:4–9.

Nehemiah had prayed about Jerusalem, and now he understood God's plan for it. The emperor said, "Yes!" God answered Nehemiah's prayer. So now he presented a list of what he needed.

Can you find his requests and what the king gave him in the wordsearch? (Find the words in bold print.)

let me go

letters to travel

and **for timber**

in the **forest**

horses to protect me

T	X	T	T	O	L
C	S	S	I	G	E
E	E	E	M	E	T
T	S	R	B	M	T
O	R	O	E	T	E
R	O	F	R	E	R
P	H	T	O	L	S

Rebuilding the walls

Have you ever been to a city that has walls around it like York, Canterbury or Chester?

Read Nehemiah 2:11–15.

City walls are an important defence against attack. Here's a map of the walls Nehemiah wanted to repair. They measured roughly four miles all the way round. It was going to be a big job. What do you think would have kept Nehemiah going?

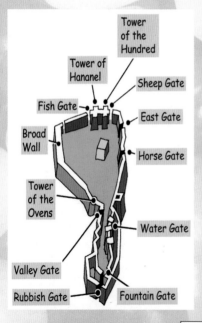

Plans into action!

Some people make you feel full of energy, so you want to join their team!

Read Nehemiah 2:16–20.

Once Nehemiah explained his plans, his team couldn't wait to get started. But then the opposition showed an interest. At first they just laughed and criticised.

Add the names of the opposition/enemies to the picture.

In the speech bubbles, write what they said and what Nehemiah replied.

Ha ha ha!

The God of heaven will

If people laugh at you because you're a Christian, be glad! It means you're a signpost, pointing to Jesus!

Ask God to make you brave enough to speak the truth and to do what's right.

Enemy action

25 July

Can you think of something you could sing a miserable song about? The song in verse 10 of today's passage is very miserable!

Read Nehemiah 4:6–15.

As if the heat, hard work and tiredness weren't enough, the builders learned from their spies that their enemies were coming to attack them.

Here's a different song that is strong and hopeful! Fill in the gaps and sing it to the tune of "The sun has got his hat on".

Our enemies can't _____ us

Hip hip hip hip hooray

Our guards have got their swords and _____

And we know how to _____

For God our Lord is _____

Hip hip hip hooray

He'll help protect our _____ and homes

We'll be OK today.

spears
hurt
mighty
walls
with us
friends
pray

Working with God

26 July

Do you know any good leaders? What do they lead? Clubs? Teams? Holidays? What makes them good leaders?

Read Nehemiah 4:16–21.

How did Nehemiah organise the builders? (verse 16)

What did the workers carry? (verse 18)

What happened at night? (verse 23)

How would you rate Nehemiah as a leader? ★ ★★ ★★★

Look at the map of the walls of Jerusalem on page 110. There was a lot of work to do, building and defending the walls. But Nehemiah didn't give up.

Crack the code using Codebreaker 3 on page 96 to find out why.

12 6 9 / 20 12 23 / 4 18 15 15 / 21 18 20 19 7 / 21 12 9 / 6 8

It was tough for Nehemiah as a leader. Pray for the leaders of your country. Ask God to help them to make wise decisions.

Finished!

The enemies of God's people had tried so hard to stop them rebuilding the walls. But what happened in the end?

Read Nehemiah 6:15–16.

The walls were finished and the enemies realised they'd been talking rubbish!

How many weeks is 52 days? Have you ever worked at anything for that long?

How do you think Nehemiah and the builders felt when the walls were complete?

Draw their faces here.

Ask God to help you stick at things that are important.

But it's not the end of the story...

What next?

Ezra, the priest and teacher, had come back to Jerusalem, too, to help the people worship God. Nehemiah shared the leadership with him.

Read Nehemiah 8:1–6.

The rebuilding was finished. Everyone had settled in. What happened next?

What's Ezra holding? What is he standing on? Complete the picture.

Try acting out what the people first did with their legs when the book was opened (verse 5); their voices after Ezra spoke (verse 6); and their whole bodies (verse 6).

Stand up, open your Bible and read **Genesis 1:1–4**. This is the beginning of the book of the Law! Now shout out, "Praise the Lord, the great God!" just as Ezra did.

cheer up!

Did you know that holiday really means 'holy day'?

Read Nehemiah 8:9–12.

Why did the people cry and feel sad? Underline what you think the reasons were:

I'm not good enough.

I forgot to buy crisps.

I failed my test.

I didn't realise that's what God's law said.

I haven't tried to obey God.

I want to go home.

I've been putting myself first.

Then what did Ezra tell the people? Fill in the missing vowels.

D _ n't b _ s _ d. _ nj _ y
y _ _ r f _ _ d _ nd dr _ nk.
Sh _ r _ w _ th _ th _ rs!
T _ d _ y _ s _ h _ l _ d _ y!

What instructions has God given you in the Bible recently? Ask him to help you to follow them, and to make you glad.

A serious matter

Saying sorry can be very hard. We should say sorry to people and God if we've done something wrong.

Read Nehemiah 9:1–3.

The party's over, and now it's time to get down to business with God. Fill in the missing words, then enter them on the grid.

They confessed their _____.

They listened for three _____.

God's law was _____ to them

They _____ the Lord

They _____.

How did they feel? Follow the arrow.

Ask God if there's anything you've done which has disappointed him. If anything comes to mind, say sorry, and ask him to help you do better next time.

Making promises

Do you always keep your promises? Here is a very solemn promise.

Read Nehemiah 10:28–29.

Seven groups of Israelites are mentioned. Who were they?

1 _____ 2 _____

3 _____ 4 _____

5 _____ 6 _____

7 _____

There's nothing wrong with foreigners! God loves everyone, from every country.

But God's people had started to accept false beliefs from people who didn't know God. It was time for a change. So what were they now promising to do?

Write it in your own words in the speech bubble.

Children were involved in making this promise, too. In the book of the Law, parents were told to help their children to learn God's laws and keep them (**Deuteronomy 6:4–9**).

Fresh start!

Sometimes people have to move house or change school. They leave their old life behind and start afresh. How might this be difficult or exciting?

Read Mark 1:14–20.

Jesus called Simon and Andrew, James and John to start afresh!

When did they follow Jesus? (Circle the right answer.)

Next week/after lunch/at once/ on Thursday/a bit later (Check your answer with verse 18.)

How do you think they felt?

Find some paper and draw a big fish. Write inside it some challenges you think Jesus is calling you to. What might you have to give up or leave behind? What might you look forward to?

Dear Jesus, it is an exciting adventure to follow you.
Help me to find my true purpose in life.

Fever cure

Have you ever had a high temperature?
Sometimes it feels as if you are never going to be well again!

Read Mark 1:29–34.

Who was ill?
Unscramble the words.

Simon's rothem-ni-wal

_____

naym lepope

_____

With a doctor you might get some medicine and have to go back for a check-up later. But Jesus heals people by the power of God's Spirit! Wow!

If you pray for people who are ill, don't forget to say thank you to God when they are well again!

Can you think of someone you know who was very ill, and now is well again? Thank God for nurses and doctors who help to heal others. Thank God for miracles, too!

Miracle health fix!

Have you ever had a broken leg?
Think of someone who has to use a wheelchair. It's frustrating when you can't walk or run about.

Read Mark 2:1–5.

This man couldn't walk. Fortunately his friends helped him out.
Imagine you are inside the crowded house when a hole appears in the ceiling and a person is lowered down!

Think about what Jesus says to him (see verse 5). Is this a surprise? Why doesn't Jesus heal him straight away?
Everyone could see he needed his legs fixed, but Jesus also knows what people need on the inside.

Jesus, you know me inside and out, and you still love me. Thank you.

Heart change

4 August

Do you remember yesterday's story?

Jesus forgave the man's sins without waiting to be asked. Wow!

But how do we know that Jesus is like God?

Read Mark 2:6–12.

So Jesus did heal the lame person after all! His body was all right again, and he was also right with God.

Fill in the speech bubbles with the missing vowels.

> G_d _s th_ _nly _n_ wh_ c_n f_rg_v_ s_ns!

> Th_ S_n _f M_n h_s _ _th_r_ty _n __rth t_ f_rg_v_ s_ns.

How did Jesus prove that he had the same power as God?

Not everyone is miraculously healed of illness or injury. But everyone can be made right with God.

How to win friends

5 August

No one wants to be friends with a cheat or a bully. Levi was like that. People also hated him because of his job, collecting taxes for the Romans.

Read Mark 2:13–17.

Levi's bad reputation didn't stop Jesus having dinner with him and showing him kindness and friendship and calling him to be one of his followers.

Think of someone you know who has cheated at something or been unkind to you. Carry a coin in your pocket to remind you to pray for them.

How can you show kindness to this person? Ask God to help you do this today.

Pain on the inside

6 August

Sometimes we have painful thoughts. Do you ever wish you could escape from the thoughts going around your head? Some people feel like that often.

Read Mark 5:1–5.

Today we read about a person who was suffering more than most. He was feeling huge pain on the inside. Some days he would hurt himself. Perhaps nobody else knew what was really troubling him. Jesus went to meet him.

Make some chains out of paper (or draw some). Write on them the things that terrify you or that trouble your friends and others in your family. Tell Jesus about them. He understands, even if nobody else does.

Keep the chains.

Let the pain out...

7 August

Who do you go to when you are hurt?

No matter how distressed we feel, Jesus is someone we can always go to for help.

Read Mark 5:6–13.

This person felt like he had a terrifying mob inside his head. How could he escape the pain?

Jesus had the power to set him completely free! Imagine what the newspapers would say the next day!

Can you make up a headline? Write it in the space.

Often the things that distress us aren't evil spirits or demons, as in this story, but unfriendly people or difficulties in everyday life.

Take the chains you made yesterday and tear them apart. As you do this, ask Jesus to take away the pain and fear.

Shout about it!

Think of a time you were bursting with good news. What did it feel like? Was it too good to keep secret?

Read Mark 5:14–20.

When the people first saw the changed man they were

_____

(verse 15).

Why do you think that was? Ask an adult you trust for their opinion as well.

When people heard his story they were _____
(verse 20).

How many people can you tell about Jesus? Make a list of your friends and neighbours. Think of something you can tell them about how Jesus has helped you. Decide to talk to one of them soon. Look out for a good moment to chat!

Jesus, having you as a friend is the best news ever! Help me to tell others so they can get to know you, too.

Praise God!

Are you ever told to be quiet? Here are some verses that tell us to shout!

Read Psalm 66:1–4.

Praise God! (English) Maladh don Tiarna! (Irish) Prys God! (Afrikaans) Preis Gott! (German) Praise God! (German)

If you can, write "Praise God!" in another language in the space. If not, write "Praise God!" in code, using Codebreaker 3 on page 96.

_____

Fill in the words to describe how great God is.

Powerful   **G**
R   **O**
A   **D**
I
S
E

What songs do you know that praise God? Hum one quietly now – or shout it. You choose!

Great things!

Do you know anyone who has done something great? What have you done that's great? (Don't be shy!) What is the greatest thing God has done for you?

Look for clues in these verses.

Read Psalm 66:5–9.

The psalm writer remembers some of the great things God did for his people. For example, God helped Moses rescue the Israelites from Egypt. (You can read about that in **Exodus 14:21–22**.)

What are two other things God does (verse 9)?

Everyone's life with God is different. What is the greatest thing God has done for you?

Why not ask this question to someone you trust, too?

Lord, thank you for doing great things for me. Help me to trust you with everything, especially

_____

_____.

Hard times? God helps!

Which of these is the odd one out and why? Paper, wood, silver, jeans and trees? (Answer on page 192.)

Read Psalm 66:10–12.

Find these words in the wordsearch:

heavy	trap	fire
burden	tested	brought
flood	silver	net

```
B P U N E T I E D
E U F L O O D H T
N T R A M P L E E
E A F D P L B A S
M A I C E E A V T
I T R A P N C Y E
E O E F S A K F D
S I L V E R S E T
B R O U G H T Y
```

Sometimes life is really hard, but what does God do for us? (Read verse 12 again.)

God has brought us to

_____.

Thank God for looking after you, even in difficult situations.

Giving thanks

12 August

Some people make promises to God when they need him. The person who wrote this psalm did. But what happens after God helps and the trouble is over?

Read Psalm 66:13–15.

Did this person forget their promise to God?

In Old Testament times, people sometimes took animals to offer at the temple to thank God. Some of the offerings became food for the priests, but not burnt offerings. As the smoke went up to the sky, it showed that the burnt offering was just for God.

God doesn't want you to make a fire or give him a bull, but ask him if you could do something special for someone as a way to thank him.

Through to God

13 August

Do you have a mobile phone? If God had one, it would always be switched on, but would we always be able to get through to him?

Psalm 66:16–19 might help to answer that.

Can't get through? Why not? Use codebreaker 3 on page 96 to see what a text from God might say. (You don't need the code for the blue numbers.)

25 / 8 12 9 9 2 / 4 / 29 /
8 18 13 8 / 7 9 13 / 25 16 /
2 / 20 12 23

_____

_____

_____

When God answered, did the psalm writer keep quiet about it? Read verse 16 again.

Have you done anything to stop you getting through to God? If so, don't ignore it. Sin is a powerful barrier that stops our prayers. Say sorry and restore the connection.

God wants the best

Do your prayers always get through to God? Does God always answer your prayers?

Read Psalm 66:20.

Can I help?

Can I play?

Why not?

Why do you think God says "yes" to some prayers and "no" to others?

The psalm writer praises God for what he did! Find two things:

God _____
_____.

God _____
_____.

Lord, thank you that you welcome me and love me and know what's best for me.

Blasphemy

Blasphemy is saying words that don't respect God.

Anyone who says they are God isn't respecting God. God is so much bigger and better than any human, so saying you're God is a bit like making fun of God – unless, of course, you are God!

Cursing God or "blaspheming his name" is very serious. Do you remember one of the Ten Commandments that talks about that? Find it in **Exodus 20:7**.

And in case you're suddenly thinking how bad someone else is for swearing, look up **Colossians 4:6** and ask yourself how good your own words are.

Don't follow strangers

Parents and teachers always tell us we shouldn't go with strangers. They say, "Stick with people you know you can trust."

Read John 10:1–6.

Jesus says sheep are like this.

They don't follow strangers who might try to steal them and they listen out for the shepherd's voice.

How good are you at recognising people's voices?

Next time your favourite TV show is on, sit with your back to the screen (or shut your eyes). How many characters can you recognise from their voices?

Jesus, help me listen most of all to your voice, telling me when things are wrong, and showing me how to live right.

This way, please!

When you go into a cinema or theatre, often there is a person who holds the door open and tells you which way to go.

Always listen to the doorkeeper!

Read John 10:7–10.

On a farm, the farmer holds open the gate for the sheep to go through.

Jesus says that he shows us the right way to God. If you choose a different gate you might lose your way.

Help the sheep to choose the right gate!

In a magazine, find a picture of a door or gate (or draw one).

Carefully tear it out and write "life" on it. Stick it on your bedroom door to remind you of Jesus' promise.

Love stronger than death

Lifeguards sometimes risk their life for others. Would you die to save a friend's life?

Read John 10:11–16.

For a shepherd in Bible times, protecting the sheep could be a matter of life and death. Use Code breaker 3 on page 96 to discover some of the dangers.

4 18 15 23 / 26 13 18 14 26 15 8

8 7 12 9 14 8 /

23 26 13 20 22 9 12 6 8 /

24 15 18 21 21 8

_____

_____

_____

Think about people who put their lives at risk for others: fire-fighters, mountain rescue teams, lifeboat crews. Think about the shepherd willing to risk his life to save the sheep. Now think about Jesus, who willingly gave up his life to save us.

Thank Jesus for loving you so much that he was willing to give up his life. Tell him your thoughts.

Freedom to choose

What decisions are you allowed to make for yourself? Is it sometimes hard to do what you know is right?

Read John 10:17–21.

What did Jesus say he had the power to do? How did the crowd react?

Jesus was killed in Jerusalem, but he could have stayed away. He knew they would try to arrest him there, but he chose to die.
It was the only way to save people. No one forced Jesus to do it. It was his choice.

Thank you, Jesus, that you chose to lay down your life to save me. When I have difficult decisions, help me to do the right thing, too.

Sing a hymn or song to remind you of what Jesus did.

Prove it!

If your friends say they have something, and you don't believe them, you might say "Prove it!" But once they show you the proof, you have to believe them!

Read John 10:22–26.

The people had seen the miracles and healings, and they had heard Jesus' teaching.

They had enough proof, but still some refused to believe.

Can you remember some things Jesus did that showed he had the power of God in him?

Make a list. See how much proof you can find!

Jesus, thank you that you came from God. Your miracles and words prove it. Please help me to trust you completely.

Just like his dad

You might hear adults say, "She is just like her mother" or "He looks like his dad". Jesus didn't look like God (because God is invisible), but see what he says about himself and God.

Read John 10:27–33.

What did Jesus say about himself and God?

(Use Codebreaker 3 on page 96. The Father = God.)

7 19 22 / 21 26 7 19 22 9 / 26 13 23 / 18 / 26 9 22 / 12 13 22

_____

_____

_____

True or false?
No one can snatch us out of Jesus' hands. **T/F**
No one can snatch us out of the Father's hands. **T/F**
Jesus and the Father are one. **T/F**

Thank you, Jesus, that these promises are true. You show us what Father God is really like!

Dear Dave

How do you know the Bible is true and not made up? Ben

Dear Ben,

That's a great question, and a very important one, too. If the Bible is made up and not true I don't want to follow it. If it is God's special book and all true, I do want to follow it! Here are a few reasons why I think it is true:

1 There are lots of things in the Bible that we know are true because of historical evidence from the time or from other people's writing.

2 Jesus read the Old Testament and treated it seriously.

3 Jesus told his friends that God the Holy Spirit would help them remember all that he had said, so I believe the New Testament is true, too!

4 When I read it, it makes sense and God speaks to me through it.

Dave

A home for the Lord

God's people had been prisoners in Babylonia for many years but now they were back in Jerusalem. Life was tough for some, while others lived in fine houses.

Read Haggai 1:1–5.

God's people had forgotten who was most important. Instead of repairing the Temple – the special place where they could worship God – they built nice houses for themselves. How do you think God felt about this?

Make a list of the three people or things that are most important to you. Be honest!

1 _____

2 _____

3 _____

Talk to God about your list. Ask him to help you remember always to put him first in your life.

Trying hard

What things have you tried to do that haven't worked out? Why do you think they went wrong?

The people were trying really hard to get it right, but something was stopping them.

Read Haggai 1:6–11 to find out what it was.

Did you find out why things were not going well for God's people in Jerusalem?

Decode the message, using Codebreaker 3 on page 96, to see the reason God gave.

14 2 / 7 22 14 11 15 22 / 18 8 / 18 13 / 9 6 18 13 8

_____

_____

_____

Loving God, we're sorry for putting the things we want before you. Help us to make you Number One in our lives.

Teamwork!

Have you ever played in a team? Imagine being on a team, working together with God!

Find out what happened when the people in Jerusalem worked together with God.

Read Haggai 1:12–15.

The team was successful because God was there with them. What did God do (verse 14)?

God inspired them, giving them enthusiasm to work on the Temple.

You might own a shirt in your favourite team's colours. What do you think God's team shirt would look like?

Thank you, God, that you ask us to play on your team. We know that when we work together with you, nothing is impossible.

(Psst! Did you know? "Enthusiasm" comes from the Greek word "enthousiazein", which means "inspired by a god".)

cheer up!

The people were rebuilding the Temple, 520 years before Jesus.

They had no diggers, cranes or cement mixers – and no power tools.

Complete the picture of how you might feel doing all that work.

The people who were building might get too tired and give up.

Read Haggai 2:1–5 to see how God encouraged them.

Do you think the memory of how glorious the temple used to be would help them to keep going?

Think of a time when you thought about giving up on something that was hard to do but God helped you get through it. Thank him for knowing you so well and for being your support.

Holy treasure

Those tired people rebuilding the Temple suddenly find out what things will be like in the future...

Read Haggai 2:6–9.

God says he will shake:

nveaeh _ _ _ _ _ _

haret _ _ _ _ _

daln _ _ _ _ and esa _ _ _

Everything is brought to the temple – all the world's treasures. This is a picture of what it means to give God our whole life.

When everyone in the world gives God everything, putting him first in their lives, there will be peace.

On a piece of foil, write the word "Peace". As you pray, look into the reflection and remember that we, too, are a treasure that belongs to God. Thank God that, when we give our lives to him, he gives us peace.

Never enough

Today God asks the people to remember the years before they started rebuilding the Temple, when some people had a good life and some had "nothing".

Read Haggai 2:15–19.

Can you find in the passage the things they wanted and what they found instead?

The Temple foundations were finished. That showed they were putting God first and God promised to bless them. When God blesses us, it means that he gives us what we need. Sometimes he gives us more than we need!

Thank you, God, that you patiently wait for us to put you first. Thanks for blessing us with all the things we need, like all the good food you give us.

Adventures together

In the first century, several adventurers travelled far spreading the message about Jesus. Paul (who wrote most of the letters in the New Testament) was one of them. He was once a persecutor of Christians, having a lot of them killed, but Jesus changed him and he wanted to tell everyone about Jesus.

One of his helpers was Timothy. He had become a Christian when he heard Paul preach. They made a good team. They set up new churches and encouraged lots of believers. Paul left Timothy in charge of the work in Ephesus, even though he was young and not very confident.

We know this because the New Testament contains two letters which Paul wrote to Timothy. Why not try reading them for yourself?

God is light

Where is the darkest place you've ever been? What did it feel like?

Read 1 John 1:5–7 to find out what the Bible says about light.

Fill in the blanks by drawing lines like this ▬▬▬ instead of the word 'light', and shade like this ● instead of the word 'darkness'.

God is _____ . There is no

_____ in him.

He sent Jesus to take away the

_____ of all the wrong things

in the world.

He wants us to live in the

_____ .

Dear God, I'm sorry for the times I live in the ● . Please help me to live in the ▬▬▬ . Amen.

All because of him

What is the middle letter of the word "sin"? That's what sin is – when we say I am going to do what I want, not what God wants.

Read 1 John 1:8 – 2:2.

Draw a sad or happy face beside these statements.

God wants to be our friend.

We all say and do wrong things.

Our sin spoils our friendship with God.

God never stops loving us.

When we sin, Jesus pleads with God to forgive us.

Are there things you need to ask God to forgive you for? Pray and tell him about them now.

Obedience = love

Unjumble the bold, red words.
God **solve** _ _ _ _ _ his people, and he wants them to **yebo** _ _ _ _ his commandments so that they can live to **spalee** _ _ _ _ _ _ him.

Read 1 John 2:3–6.

Who does verse 6 tell us to live like? Jot down some of the ways you could be like Jesus in the way you live and then use your ideas in the prayer below.

_____

_____

_____

_____

_____

Please God, help me to obey you and be like Jesus in the way I live. Please help me to be more

_____ .

Amen.

Spoilt world

When God created the world it was perfect, but because of people's sin it has been spoiled. What are some of the things that spoil it? Write them around the globe.

Read 1 John 2:15–17.

What's the warning in these verses? (Cross out the wrong answers.)

Love the world./Do not love the world.

What does it mean?

We should not love the world God created./We should not love the bad things that spoil God's world.

Read **1 John 2:17** again and then pray and ask God to help you to love him and do what he wants.

Stay close to Jesus

Have you ever felt frightened or nervous or unsure what to do? What a difference it makes if someone says, "Stay close to me"!

Read 1 John 2:28–29.

The Bible says, "remain in union with Jesus", or "stay one in your hearts with him", but it means the same thing! Imagine Jesus saying these words to you:

> ## Stay close to me!

How do we stay close to Jesus? Turn this page upside down to find out!

Please, God, help me to stay close to Jesus whatever I do each day. Amen.

1 Keep reading the Bible to find out what God wants.
2 Go to church or a Christian group if possible.
3 Talk to God at any time.

God's children

Wouldn't it be great to have a really famous relation?

Read 1 John 3:1–3.

God – the amazing God of the Bible – loves us and calls us his children!

In the shape below, write or draw what you want to say to God about that. If it makes you feel like dancing or singing, do that instead!

Here are some things that parents do for their children and God does for us.

Protect (**Psalm 27:1**)

Forgive (**Psalm 32:1**)

Provide (**Psalm 23:1**)

Can you think of others?

Thank God that he loves us so much that he lets us be his children.

Love in action

5 September

Action! That's what a film director says when he wants something to happen. That's what God tells us, too!

Read 1 John 3:16–18.

It's no good saying we love God if we don't do anything about it! God wants to see us in action, doing things that show we love him.

Read verse 17 again. John talks about people in need. That might be someone at your school, or living near you. Perhaps you could be kind to them, or share something with them, or… what else?

Think! Who do you know who is in need?
What could you do for them?
Pray!

God is love

6 September

If you see this, what do you think of?

Love is mentioned in the Bible loads of times, but it's about God's love and what he has done for us, not mushy, sloppy stuff!

Read 1 John 4:7–12.

How many times is the word "love", "loves" or "loved" mentioned in these six verses?

(Answer on page 192.)

God takes love very seriously. Check out how much God loves us – find **1 John 3:16** (from yesterday's verses) and **John 3:16**.

Pray and ask God to help you love other people. Tell God about some people you know and try to think of ways to show love to them.

Living with God

🗒️ **7 September**

Today's verses are about God living with us – as if we've said to him, "Make yourself at home". Awesome!

Read 1 John 4:13–16.

Can you join the right answer to each question?

Question

If we "live in union" with God, what happens (verse 13)?

What should we tell others (verse 14)?

What can we know and believe (verse 16)?

Answer

God sent Jesus to be the Saviour of the world.
God loves us!
We have the Holy Spirit to be with us and help us.

Even if you don't understand everything in these verses, thank God that he loves you and wants to be "at home" with you!

Loveable or not?

🗒️ **8 September**

Do you love God? Why? How do you show it?

Read 1 John 4:19–21.

Do you have any brothers or sisters? What about cousins, friends or neighbours?
Draw some of their faces and name them.

Is it easy to love them? **Yes/No**
We show we love God when we love others.

Ask God to help you love each person you've drawn and named, even when it isn't easy. Pray for each of them.

Why not make a card telling someone you love them?

Winning together

Can you remember when someone helped you to do something really hard? That's what happens with God and us – he wants us to work together, God and all his children!

Read 1 John 5:1–5.

Do you always find it easy to obey God?

Lots of people in the Bible had trouble doing what God asked them to do. Can you think of any?

Obeying God might be hard, but it's possible. How? (Look at verses 3–5 again.)

Lord God, sometimes it's hard to obey you. Please help me to want to. Help me to remember that I'm your child and that you will help me to do anything you ask me to do.

Tuned in or tuned out

Do people always listen carefully when you're talking? Does God tune out when we talk too much? What if we keep asking him for things?

Read 1 John 5:13–15.

If God gives us what we ask for, can we make a list? Hmmm – not quite! Verse 14 says, "...when we ask for what pleases him"

We should ask God for things he wants for us. We should pray for things that will help us.

15 12 5 22 _ _ _ _,

12 25 22 2 _ _ _ _ and

8 22 9 5 22 _ _ _ _ _ him.

Use Codebreaker 3 on page 96 to find out what to ask God for.)

Dear God, you want us to love, obey and serve you. Thank you that we're not on our own – the Holy Spirit helps us. Amen.

(Psst! We listen to God with our spirit, not with our ears.)

The Sword

The sword is mentioned in the Bible more times than any other weapon.

In **Hebrews 4:12** God's words are said to be "sharper than any two-edged sword". The original two-edged swords were more like daggers – they could easily do your enemy a lot of damage! So why are God's words like a sword?

A sword can go deep inside the body (yuk!) and in the same way, God's words have the power to show us what is really going on in our lives – even what our thoughts are like. As it says in **Hebrews 4:13**: "Nothing is hidden from God."

If you cut yourself, it can be very painful. In the same way, when God shows us things through his Word, sometimes it can be quite uncomfortable, too! God does it to help us change and become more like Jesus.

Keep asking God to speak to you as you read your Bible – there's no telling what you'll discover!

Lights from the sky

After Jesus had risen from the dead and gone back to heaven, his disciples began to tell everyone the good news about him. One man, Saul, hated Christians and was determined to have them all arrested.

Read Acts 9:1–6.

Fill in the missing parts of the story.
Saul was going to _____
when a _____
flashed from _____.

Saul _____ to the ground. He heard a voice saying, "Why are you _____ me?"

Saul asked, " _____
_____?"

The voice replied, "I am
_____."

Ask God to show himself to someone you know who doesn't love him.

In the dark!

Do you ever get so surprised by things that you open your mouth but no words come out? What happened to Saul after his surprise meeting with Jesus?

Read Acts 9:7–9.

What did Saul's friends hear?

What did they see?

What did Saul see?

How long did he stay like that?

Saul had a lot to think about. He realised he had been wrong all along. Now he understood who Jesus really was.

How do you think he felt?

Do you understand who Jesus really is? Tell him what you think.

A difficult task

Can you remember a time when you've been asked to do something that you thought would be really scary? This happened to a man in Damascus. What was his name?

Read Acts 9:10–14.

Are these statements true or false?
God called Ananias in a vision. **T/F**
He was to go to Front Street. **T/F**
He was to look for Saul in Peter's house. **T/F**
Saul was praying. **T/F**
Saul was expecting him. **T/F**
(Answers on page 192.)

Do you think Ananias was happy to do what God asked? Why/why not? (Verses 13–14 may help.)

Dear Lord, sometimes following you is hard. Help me to do what you want even if it seems scary, especially when _____ _____.

God's plans

Even though Ananias was scared, God still wanted him to talk to Saul.

Read Acts 9:15–19.

God had big plans for Saul. Find three groups of people Saul would talk to about Jesus:

1 _____
2 _____
3 _____

Find three things that happened when Ananias visited Saul:

1 _____
2 _____
3 _____

God uses ordinary (and sometimes scared) people to do his work.

Are you willing to let God use you? Talk to him about your thoughts. (Psst: Gentiles are any people who are not Jews.)

What a change!

Question: What do caterpillars and tadpoles have in common?

Answer: They both change into something completely different.

Saul had totally changed, too.

Read Acts 9:19–22.

Once Saul had tried to destroy followers of Jesus (look at **Acts 8:3**), but now what was he preaching about Jesus? Use Codebreaker 3 on page 96 to find out:

17 22 8 6 8 / 18 8 / 7 19 22 / 8 12 13 / 12 21 / 20 12 23

_____
_____
_____

It was meeting Jesus that changed Saul. Can you think of ways in which you might have changed since you met Jesus?
(Psst! Saul was later known as Paul.)

Thank you, Jesus, for changing me. Help me to keep growing more like you every day.

Kill him!

17 September

Since meeting Jesus, everything in Saul's life seemed to have turned upside down. What was happening to him now?

Read Acts 9:23–25.

Once Saul had tried to kill Christians, now the Jews were plotting to kill him! Why?

The people Saul once hated had now become his friends.

Join the dots to find out how they helped him escape from Damascus.

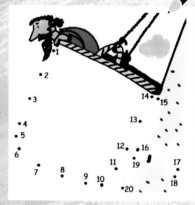

Thank you, God, for Christian friends who have helped me, especially _____.

Bible challenge

18 September

How well do you know your Bible? Do you know any of it off by heart?

Challenge yourself to learn these three verses. See if you can find them in your Bible. Think about them as you read them. What do they tell you about God? What do they say about you?

What do you want to say to God about them?

All things are done according to God's plan and decision; and God chose us to be his own people.
Ephesians 1:11 (GNB)

My grace is all you need, for my power is greatest when you are weak.
2 Corinthians 12:9 (GNB)

Jesus said, "I am the way, the truth, and the life; no one goes to the Father except by me."
John 14:6 (GNB)

Jesus the storyteller

Everybody enjoys a good story! If a TV programme stops in the middle of the action, you want to know what will happen next! Where do you enjoy stories? In books? In films? What are your favourite stories?

Read Mark 4:1–3.

Jesus knew people liked a good story, and he was a good storyteller. Circle where Jesus told his stories.

in a house

by the lakeshore

on TV

in the synagogue

What book or TV programme have you enjoyed recently? Think of two things you have learned about life from the story.

Dear God, help me learn new things from the stories in the Bible.

Attitude?

Have you ever sown seeds which grew into beautiful plants? It is not easy – you can't just do it any old how!

In today's story, some seeds didn't grow much. Look out for why not.

Read Mark 4:3–9.

Jesus is not teaching about farming! He used this story to teach about people's attitudes to God's Word.

How many times did Jesus tell them to listen?

We have to listen, too! We can't learn the lesson any old how! We have to pay attention!

Find an empty jar, and put a handful of seeds in it. Birdseed or rice will do. (Or draw seeds falling to the ground.) Ask God to help you listen to him and to others.

Too tough to handle?

21 September

Have you ever fed the birds in the park?

Throw seeds on the footpath and in a moment the birds peck it up and it's gone! There's no way those seeds will grow. The path is too hard.

Read Mark 4:13–15.

Like the footpath, some people are "hardhearted".

They want their own way. They won't let God's Word challenge their life, and change their attitude and what they do. What about you?

Are you sometimes stubborn, when you should do what you are told? Or uncaring when you should be kind? God says: "Change your attitude!"

Take your jar (from yesterday) and put a shoelace in it — to remind you of the footpath. (Or draw a path on your seed picture.)

Ask God to help you have a good attitude.

Rocky problems?

22 September

Have you ever tried to dig the ground, but found rocks underneath? Rocky soil is not good for plants!

Read Mark 4:16–17.

Shallow people don't think very deeply about anything. They want easy answers to all life's problems. But if we want to keep on living God's way, sometimes it will be difficult!

What are some of the struggles you face this week?

Problem at school:

_____

Problem at home:

_____

Problem living God's way:

_____

God cares about you and understands your struggles.

Take your jar of seeds and put some stones in it. (Or draw rocks on your picture.) As you do this, tell God about the troubles you face, and ask him to help you.

Worrying?

23 September

Imagine a friend shows you their new toy: an expensive mobile phone, the latest computer game, or a flashy watch. Do you wish you had one, too?

Read Mark 4:18–19.

Some people think having lots of things will make them happy. But things might get stolen, or broken, or lost. Having lots of things means there is more to worry about! Some people worry too much and don't have time for God.

Take your jar and add some weeds to it. (Or draw weeds on your picture.) As you do this, think about some of the toys and games you wish you had. Tell God you don't really need these things, and ask for help not to worry about them anymore.

Grow fruit!

24 September

Look at your jar of seeds (or picture) again. Think about the different places the seed fell. Which are you like?

Read Mark 4:20.

Seeds in good soil can grow and produce good fruit.

For our life to produce good fruit we need to _____ and _____ God's message.

Is your life growing "good fruit"?

What attitudes and characteristics do you want to change?

Being kinder to others/stopping swearing/having more patience?

You decide! Write it on a piece of paper and put it in the jar with the seeds. (Or write it on your picture.) Then ask God to help you.

Dear God, I accept your word. Let it change my attitude, character and friendships.

Stop it!

25 September

Peter really knew what people are like!

Read 1 Peter 2:1.

Draw lines from STOP and START to the right things:

STOP	START

Being hateful

Saying good things

Being sincere

Fooling people

Being kind

Being jealous

Saying cruel things

Fill in the speech bubbles with good things to say to others:

Dear God, help me to stop doing and saying wrong things. Amen.

Growing with God

26 September

If you were really thirsty which of these would you drink? Circle your choice:

Cola   orange juice

water   milk

What does Peter say about how a baby drinks?

Read 1 Peter 2:2–3.

What would happen if a new baby didn't drink milk?

God wants us to grow in our faith as we get to know him better. What is one important thing we can remember to help us grow?

Unravel the words from verse 3.

who dogo het droL leryal si

_____

Be quiet and still, just like a baby who has had enough to drink and who feels safe and comfortable. Think of all the good things God has given you and done for you.

Stones with Jesus

Peter moves on from the picture of a baby to the picture of a wall. What does he say about this building or spiritual house made up of living stones?

Read 1 Peter 2:4–5.

You might imagine that the walls are made up of jumping bricks. Really Peter is saying that all the people in the wall are important... and who is at the centre?

Fill in the name on the centre stone and then your name and the names of friends and family who love Jesus on the other stones.

J_ _ _ _

What are the builders like who ignored the best stone?

Read 1 Peter 2:7–8. Ask God to help you always to trust Jesus, just like a living stone.

Living in the light

Do you sometimes think that you don't matter to anyone, even to God? Peter makes a list of some fantastic things that God has done for us. What are they?

Read 1 Peter 2:9–10.

Tick the true things and cross out the untrue ones:

☐ You are chosen by God.

☐ You are not special to him.

☐ God has treated you with kindness.

☐ We must not tell what God has done for us.

☐ God has brought you into darkness.

☐ God has brought you into light.

Dear God, thank you that I can live in the light because you have chosen me.

Jokes page

What do you get if you cross a football team with an ice cream?

Aston Vanilla

What is green and hairy and jumps up and down?

A gooseberry doing ballet

Why did the chicken cross the park?

To get to the other slide

Why did the banana go to the doctor?

It wasn't peeling well.

What did the traffic lights say to the lorry?

Don't look now, I'm changing.

What goes zzub... zzub... zzub...?

A bee flying backwards.

Why did the polo go to school?

Because he wanted to be a smartie

What bird prepares food?

A cook-coo

What do you get if you cross a fish with two elephants?

Swimming trunks.

We are being watched!

29 September

Who watches you? Circle them and add others:

people who dislike you

teachers   **parents**

friends   **neighbours**

_____

Sometimes people watch you because they are concerned for your safety. Sometimes it is because they want to catch you out or they wonder why you do certain things!

Read 1 Peter 2:12.

Peter warns us that we are being watched. Put what he says in your own words.

_____
_____
_____

Why do you think others may accuse you of doing wrong?

Ask God to help you always to do what is right, whoever may be watching.

Respecting leaders

30 September

Sometimes it is hard to respect people, especially if others around us are being disrespectful. Who does Peter say these believers should respect?

Read 1 Peter 2:13–17.

Cross out every W, X and Z.

XXTHWEEZMPWEXROZR

_____

GOXZVERWZNXOZRWZS

_____

XEVZXERXYWWOZNXE

_____

XGZOWWD

_____

The Emperor and governors had been appointed by God to make sure that people lived together happily and in safety, even though they may not have done this very well! God wants us to respect our leaders too.

Who are the leaders...

in your church? _____

in your school? _____

in your country? _____

Ask God to help them do a good job.

Bad news and good news

No one likes bad news, but good news makes us happy.

Read Genesis 6:5–10.

Draw a sad face beside the bad news.

Draw a happy face beside the good news.

- The people God created became very wicked.
- God was sorry he had made them.
- God decided to punish them.
- Noah was the only good man.
- God was pleased with Noah.
- Noah was God's friend.

God is sad when we don't live his way. How does that make you feel?

God loves us and wants to forgive us so that we can be his friends! How does that make you feel?

If you are sorry for the times when you let God down, tell him now.

Amazing God!

Do you think today's Bible verses will be good or bad news?

Read Genesis 6:11–22 to find out.

There was some good news, but who for? Check out verse 18.

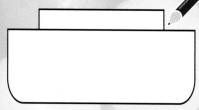

Inside the boat outline, draw and label the man whose family was safe. Then draw a few of the animals.

The boat Noah built was HUGE! Next time you're on your way to school, take 266 strides. That's roughly how long it was!

Thank God for his amazing plan to save Noah, his family and all the animals.

An amazing rescue plan

Circle the weather you like most.

Can you make any of them happen? Y/N

God can!

Read Genesis 7:11–16.

God meant what he said when he told Noah he would punish everyone who had disobeyed him.

God set up a rescue plan for Noah and his family.

Why did God rescue Noah and his family?

Check out verses 1 and 5.

Do you think it's important that it was God who shut the door? (See verse 16.)

Noah lived God's way. Think of one thing you can do that will please God. Now ask him to help you to do it.

Waiting...

Are you any good at waiting for something to happen?

Noah had to wait a long time before he could come out of the ark.

Read Genesis 8:1–12.

How many days did the water take to go down?

☐ 120   ☐ 150   ☐ 130

When did the boat come to rest on a mountain?

☐ On the 17th day of the seventh month.

☐ On the tenth day of the eighth month.

When did Noah send out a raven?

☐ After 50 days.

☐ After 40 days.

(Answers on page 192.)

Even though Noah had to wait a long time, what happened? Read the first few words of verse 1.

God didn't forget Noah. Thank him that he never forgets us, wherever we are and whatever we are doing!

A new start

If you make a mistake, it's great to have a new start. God gave the world a new start after the flood.

Read Genesis 8:13–22.

The flood was over. What did God say Noah should do?

_____

_____

_____

Noah offered a sacrifice to say "thank you" to God in a special way. What did God think about it?

_____

_____

What did God promise?

Never again_____

_____ .

Kneel down and say sorry to God for wrong things you do. Now stand up and raise your arms. Thank God for his promise never to destroy the earth again.

Are you sure?

In the first century after Jesus' birth, new Christians had lots of questions. Hebrews was written to help them understand who Jesus was and what being a follower of him was all about.

One question they had was: What is faith? Any ideas?

Read Hebrews 11:1–3.

Unscramble the words:
Faith means being...
ures fo ingths ew opeh rof
terniac fo thgnis ew tan'c ese

_____

_____

_____

_____

Use a red pen to circle the words that show faith doesn't just mean "maybe" or "possibly".

Dear God, please help my faith to get stronger as I learn more about you.

Trust and obey

Have you ever been on a bus or a train that's gone to the wrong place? We trust the driver to go where he says he's going!

Read Hebrews 11:7–10.

What did God ask Noah to do?
Build a b _ _ _.
What did God tell Abraham to do?
Go to a new c _ _ _ _ _ _.
Noah and Abraham obeyed because they had f _ _ _ _ in G _ _.

Noah and Abraham thought God was worth trusting and obeying. Why did they trust him?
Can you think of someone else who obeyed God without knowing where he would lead them?

Why can you trust God?
Tell God your thoughts.

Impossible or not?

Are all these things impossible?

Read Hebrews 11:11–12.

God had promised Abraham and Sarah that their family would be as big as the number of stars in the sky… but they were too old to have children.
What did Abraham do?
Cross out the Xs and Zs to find out.

> HXE TZRXUZSXTZXEXD GZOXD TZO
> KXEZEXP HZIXS PXRZOXMZIXSZEXS

And did God keep his promise?
Yes/No (Look back to verse 12 to check.)

God can do impossible things!

Dear God, Abraham and Sarah trusted you even when things looked impossible. Help me to have faith like theirs.

whose side are you on?

9 October

Which would you rather be: rich and comfortable or wandering in the desert for 40 years? What did Moses think?

Enjoy sin

Read Hebrews 11:23–27.

Fit the scattered words from around the page into the spaces to find out what Moses decided to do:

He preferred to _____ rather than _____ (verse 25).

He knew that suffering for the _____ was better than the _____ (verse 26).

Which would you rather do: stay on God's side even when it's really hard, or give up when it's tough? Why?

Messiah

Lord God, sometimes it's hard to stay close to you, especially when _____ Please help me.

treasures of Egypt

suffer with God's people

Astonishing scenes

10 October

What's the most amazing thing you've ever done? Compare that to the incidents on this list...

Read Hebrews 11:32–34.

Match the two halves of the sentences to reveal the astonishing happenings:

shut the	fierce fires
put out	became strong
escaped being	mouths of lions
weak	armies of foreigners
defeated	killed by the sword

Because of their faith, God helped the people to do amazing things. Use a mirror to find out another important thing:

God made promises to them because they did right.

Will you be remembered for doing what's right? Talk to God about how he can help you.

Don't give up

Have you ever felt like you're the only Christian around? You are not alone!

Read Hebrews 12:1–3.

What's the best way to keep going as a Christian?
Fill in the spaces.
Get rid of everything that

_____.

Get rid of sin which

_____.

Run with determination the

_____.

Keep your eyes fixed on

_____.

Jesus suffered lots of pain and hatred – but he didn't give up.

Dear Lord, sometimes it's really hard to be a Christian especially when _____.
When I feel like giving up, help me to remember what Jesus did for me.

Make a cross-shaped bookmark to remind you of what Jesus did.

Use your senses!

Are your teachers mean or generous with praise? How often do they say, "Well done!", "That's great!" or "Brilliant"?
Are you mean or generous with your praise to God?

Read Psalm 103:1–2.

If you are allowed, take a walk outside and list all the things that you can see and hear, touch and smell.
Praise God for each thing he has lovingly created for our enjoyment.

Fill in the spaces below to create your own praise prayer.
Praise God for the sight of

_____.

For the sound of

_____.

For the smell of

_____.

For the feel of

_____.

For the taste of

_____.

Praise God with all your being and all your senses.

What God does

Have you ever written a thank you letter?

In **Psalm 103** King David shows how thankful he is for all the good things God does.

Read Psalm 103:3–7.

Which of the following things does King David mention in his psalm?

- [ ] God forgives all my sins.
- [ ] God heals all my diseases.
- [ ] God blesses me with kindness, love and mercy.
- [ ] God brings justice to those who are mistreated or oppressed.
- [ ] God fills my life with good things and provides for my needs.

Did you tick all of them?

Why not write a thank you letter to God? Thank him for the good things he does and the good things he has given you.

If you don't want to write the words down, just say them in your heart.

What God's like

What is your best friend like? Circle all the words that describe them...

kind   loving   forgiving

loyal   patient   thoughtful

fun   interesting

Read Psalm 103:8–10.

No matter how warmly you have described your friend, it would be hard to improve on David's description of God.

Read the verses and then cross out the two false sentences.

God gets angry quickly.

God is always full of love.

God doesn't nag and scold all the time.

God gives people the punishment they deserve.

God doesn't pay us back for our sins.

Talk to God just as you talk to your best friend. Tell him anything you are worried about, anything you want to thank him for, anything that you are sorry about.

God's forgiveness

🗓 **15 October**

Have you said sorry to anyone recently?

Did the other person turn away angrily?

Or did they say, "I forgive you. Let's start again"? It's good to be forgiven, isn't it?

Read Psalm 103:11–13.

We have rewritten today's verses. Can you spot what's changed?

As high as Mount Everest is above sea level so great is God's love.

As far as Great Britain is from Australia so far does God remove our sins.

As good friends are kind to each other so is God kind to all those who respect him.

Rewrite verse 12 in your own words:

As far as _____

is from _____

so far does God take our sins from us.

Thank God that when we say sorry he forgives us and removes all the wrong things we have done so that we can make a clean start.

With God for ever

🗓 **16 October**

Have you ever picked up a dandelion clock and blown away the fluff? It all disappears in the wind and you are left with a bare stalk.

Read how David, the psalmist, says that people are a bit like that in **Psalm 103:14–18.**

People don't last for ever, but something else does. Circle the right answer:

God's creatures   God's love

God's creation   God's flowers

If God's love lasts for ever, that means he always loves those who follow him, during their life on earth and throughout their life in heaven too – in other words eternally!

You can read this prayer again and again!

Eternal God, thank you that your love lasts for ever and ever.

Praise him again!

Do you have a favourite pop song? Some songs repeat the same line again and again, don't they? King David's psalms were the hit songs of his day. He often repeats a word or phrase several times.

Read Psalm 103:19–22.

How many times does David use the words "Praise the Lord!" or "Praise your Lord!" in these verses?

Who does he think should praise the Lord?

Check the verses and write in the vowels.

_ ng _ ls

H _ _ v _ nly p _ w _ rs or

th _ _ s _ nds wh _ s _ rv _

_ ll G _ d's cr _ _ t _ r _ s

D _ v _ d h _ ms _ lf

Write or draw your own four reasons to say "Praise the Lord!"

Make way

When Jesus grew up he began his time of teaching and telling people about the kingdom of God. In the next few days we are going to look at how it all started.

Read Matthew 3:1–6.

John's clothes were made of

_____,

he wore a _____

around his waist, and he ate

_____ and _____

(verse 4). Can you imagine that?

John told the people that they had to make a straight road for the Lord. He didn't mean that they had to build an actual road for the Lord to travel on. He was talking about making a way in their lives for the Lord to come to them.

Is there anything in your life that would block the way and stop the Lord coming to you?
Talk with God about it now. Ask God to help you clear the way.

No pretending

When John told people to get ready for the Lord there were some people who thought that they were perfect and did not need to change. Let's see what John had to say to them...

Read Matthew 3:7–12.

John tells everybody that it's no use pretending to be perfect. People who have really turned from their sins and turned to God will show it. How?

B 3re  tchy

3rey hl

Is there some way that you pretend to be perfect when you're not? That can stop us from welcoming God.

Dear God, thank you that we can turn to you at any time and you will give us the power to turn away from sin like Jesus did.

Listen for God

John was baptising people in the river to get them ready for when Jesus started to teach. He's about to get a surprise!

Read Matthew 3:13–17.

God spoke from heaven. What did he say?

This is... (Use Codebreaker 4 on page 96.)

📦 3 🐦 5 / 📦 5 🐦 3 📦 4 /

🌿 4 🌿 5 🌿 1 ☂ 3 /

☂ 4 📦 5 📦 4

_____

_____

God speaks to us, too, but it's not usually through our ears with a voice from heaven. Sometimes it's through our spirit. We need to "tune in" if we want to hear.

Try it! A dove reminds us of God being in our lives – his Spirit lives in us. Set aside some time and find a quiet place. Look at the picture of the dove, be quiet with God and let him speak to you.

He's at it again

Do you remember how the snake tempted Eve in the garden? Jesus was also tempted to do things that were wrong. Let's find out what they were...

Read Matthew 4:1–4.

Circle the right answer:

Jesus went without food for 4/40/400 days.

The devil told Jesus to turn trees/water/stones into bread.

Jesus told the devil that we need every order/story/word that God speaks.

Which are your favourite verses and stories in the Bible? What do they tell you about God?

Loving God, thank you that you give us your Word to help us in our lives and to help us know you better.

Powerful words

Remembering God's own words is the best way to make sure we live right.

Jesus used some of God's words from the Bible when he was tempted.

Read Matthew 4:5–11.

Can you find the verses Jesus used?

The Scripture says:

_____

(verse 7).

_____

(verse 10).

Remembering Bible verses can often be quite hard, but if you do there are always rewards!

Read over these Bible words Jesus used a few times and try to remember them without looking.

Who could you challenge to learn them with you? Ask each other in a week.

Dear God, thank you for your words in the Bible. Please help me to love them and use them and remember them.

The message

Jesus has been baptised and has refused to give in to temptation. He is obeying God. He is ready to start telling people the good news.

Read Matthew 4:12–17.

Six hundred years earlier, Isaiah wrote about Jesus and said that he would go to Galilee. This shows that God's word is true. Isaiah said:

The people who live in
_ _ _ _ _ _ _ _ will see a bright
_ _ _ _ _. For those who live in
death a _ _ _ _ _ will _ _ _ _ _.

With paper, make a lampshade to go around a torch. Before you attach it, write the word "Jesus" on it in bold colourful letters.

Thank you, God, that we are ready for the light of Jesus to shine in our world. Amen.

Famous 40s

Here are just a few famous 40s.

The number 40 is used many times in the Bible. Some Bible experts believe 40 is a "round number", that 40 years means a generation, or the time before the children become the leaders.

It rained for 40 days and 40 nights in Noah's time (**Genesis 7:4**).

Moses was 40 when he ran away from Egypt (**Acts 7:23**). He was in Midian for 40 years (**Acts 7:30**) and on the mountain with God for 40 days (**Exodus 24:18**).

The people of Israel were in the wilderness for 40 years (**Joshua 5:6**).

The spies were in Canaan for 40 days (**Numbers 13:25**).

In Jonah's time, the people of Nineveh were given 40 days to repent (**Jonah 3:4**).

And how many days did Jesus go without food before he was tempted? (See **Matthew 4:2**.)

"Make them miserable"

More than a thousand years before Jesus was born, Joseph's family moved to Egypt during a famine. They settled there and had many descendants, called the Israelites or Hebrews.

Read Exodus 1:8–14.

The Egyptian king made a plan to get rid of the Israelites. Cross out the wrong words in his message to the people.

> The Israelites have become too strong and powerful/ heavy/happy for us. If there's a war they might run away/ sing songs/fight against us. Let's make them into dancers/ hardworking slaves/tax collectors.

Did the king's plan work? (See verse 12.)

The Egyptians bullied the Israelites because they were afraid of them. Talk with God about any bullying you know of. Talk about it with an adult you trust, too.

Real fear

Fear made the king turn the Israelites into slaves. See what it did next...

Read Exodus 1:15–22.

True or false?

The king told the women to kill all baby boys. **T/F**

The women did what the king said. **T/F**

All the boys died. **T/F**

God was kind to the two women. **T/F**

The Israelites increased and grew stronger. **T/F** (Answers on page 192.)

Why did the women disobey the king (verse 17)?
Some Bibles say that the women "feared" God. Do you think this means that they were scared of God, or that they respected God? Or both?

Kneel down or bow your head and think about how powerful God is.

Hide him, quick!

27 October

Can you find the pairs?

How do you protect a baby?

Read Exodus 2:1–6.

Join the dots to see where the woman hid her baby.

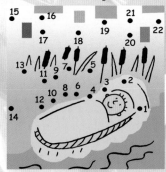

How did each of these people or things protect the baby?

His mother   The basket

His sister   The princess

Who protects and looks after you?

Talk with God about times you feel in need of his protection.

From slave to prince

28 October

Have you ever moved house? This baby did – and what a change!

Read Exodus 2:7–10.

Who looked after the baby first?

His m _ _ _ _ _ (who was a Hebrew slave).

Then who did he live with?

A p _ _ _ _ _ _ _.

What did she call him? M _ _ _ _.

Moses went from a slave's house to the palace!

Do you think God was with Moses in his mother's home? What about in the palace? Do you think God is with you, whatever your home is like?

In the house shape write the names of everyone you live with. Ask God to protect each person.

A dreadful deed

Moses was now an Egyptian prince but it didn't stop him remembering that he was really a Hebrew.

Read Exodus 2:11–15.

Put the events in the right order by numbering the squares:

☐ Moses ran away.

☐ Moses saw two Hebrews fighting.

☐ Moses killed the Egyptian. People found out.

☐ Moses saw an Egyptian beat up a Hebrew.

Moses' life had been complicated, but there was no excuse for what he did. He knew he'd done the wrong thing, too.

Dear God, I'm sorry for things I do wrong, especially things like

_____.

Please forgive me. When I get angry, help me to do the right thing.

God cares

When things look hopeless, there's something worth doing.

Read Exodus 2:23–25.

The Israelites cried out to God for help.

What did God do? Fit the correct words in the spaces:

remembered/felt sorry for/heard

God _____ the Israelites cry out.

God _____ his covenant promise.

God _____ his people.

A covenant is a contract, a promise. Years before this, God had promised Abraham that his family would become a great nation in a land of their own. God promised to bless Abraham's family for ever. In fact, God said he'd bless the whole world through Abraham!

Say thank you to God because he keeps his promises. Talk to him about anything that's troubling you.

prayer time

We can talk to God at any time and in any place. Do you find that you talk to God more when you need help or are in trouble? One of the best things God does is to give us peace inside. What's worrying us may still be there but it stops being such a big thing! God helps us to trust him. In Philippians 4:6-7 Paul tells us how to pray. He says:

"Don't worry about anything, but pray about everything. With thankful hearts offer up your prayers and requests to God. Then, because you belong to Christ Jesus, God will bless you with peace that no one can completely understand. And this peace will control the way you think and feel."

When you need peace inside, start by thanking God for his love and care, then ask him to look after you and to answer your prayer. Give God's promise a go!

Voice from a bush

Do you remember the bad thing that Moses had done?

Find out why he was suddenly very afraid.

Read Exodus 3:1–6.

Can you find six differences between the two pictures? (Answers on page 192)

Moses was afraid because God is holy. Holy means to be pure or set apart. God is holy – pure goodness. There is nothing bad in God at all.

Take off your shoes and sing a worship song, or do something that shows you know how holy God is.

Who? Me?

2 November

The manager of your country's football team has just called and asked you to play in the World Cup team. What will you say?

Read Exodus 3:7–12.

God had a rescue plan for the Israelites and he wanted Moses to be part of it. What did Moses think about that?

Crack the code to reveal their conversation. Use Codebreaker 4 on page 96.

God: 🔷4/ 🌿1 📦3/ ☂4🌿5📦4🌿4🔷4📦4🔷2/ 🐿5📦5🐿1

Moses: 🔷3📦5🐿3/ 🌿3🌿1📦4/ 🔷4/ 🌿4📦5/ 🔷4☂5

God: 🔷4/ 🐿3 🔷4📦2📦2/ 🌿2🌿5/ 🐿3🔷4☂5🔷3/ 🐿5📦5🐿1

Moses was surprised that God wanted to use him. Does it surprise you to know that God wants to use you in his plans for the world?

God is...

3 November

What's your name? What are you usually called? Does your name describe what you are like? What's God's name?

Read Exodus 3:13–15.

"I AM" seems a strange name for God, but it shows that God has always existed and always will.

Make your own "colour in the shape with a dot" puzzle. Draw a circle on a sheet of paper. Write "I AM" in bubble writing and put a small dot in each shape. Add other shapes. Ask someone to do the puzzle to discover what God said his name was.

Can you think of any other names God uses to describe himself? Verse 15 will give you a start.

Thank you, God, that you were, you are, and you always will be. Thank you that you never change.

God in action

There are some things we can't do on our own.

The Israelites couldn't escape from Egypt by themselves, but God was on their side.

Read Exodus 3:16–20.

Cross out all the Xs and Zs to see what God said he would do.

X1Z WXIZLXL XUZSĊE

_____

ZMXY ZMXIZGXHZTXY

_____

ZPXOZWXEZR

_____

God wants to help us, he has the power to help us and he does help us!

Think of a place in God's world where people need his help. Ask God to use his mighty power to make their lives better.

Sticks and snakes

Imagine that you bumped into your favourite sports star or singer. You tell your friends, but they don't believe you. How could you prove it?

Read Exodus 4:1–5.

Moses didn't think anyone would believe that God had sent him. How would he prove it?

What did God tell him to do? Draw the final two frames of the story.

What did God say this miracle would do (verse 5)?

Is there anything you need to do that you're unsure or worried about? Ask God for his help.

GO! NO!

6 November

Have you ever made excuses to get out of doing something hard?

Read Exodus 4:10–17.

Even though God promised to be with him, Moses still wasn't keen to do what God asked.

Finish the script with these words: someone else, speaking, words, be

Moses: No! I'm no good at

_____.

God: Go! I will _____ with you and give you the _____.

MOSES: No! Please send

_____.

Why do you think Moses said, "No"?

Why do you think God got angry (verse 14)?

But God didn't give up on Moses. Use the first letter of each picture to find out who he sent to help.

Thank you, God, for being patient and not giving up on me.

Why should I?

7 November

What might happen if someone took no notice of these messages?

DANGER THIN ICE

(30)

Wait for me before you cross the road.

Read Exodus 5:1–9.

Moses and Aaron went to the king with a message from God. What was it? (Fill in the missing vowels.)

L _ t my p _ _ pl _ g _.
What did the king reply?
Wh _ _ s th _ s L _ rd?
_ w _ ll n _ t l _ t
_ srael g _ !
What happened when Moses and Aaron asked again (verses 4–9)?

Because the king ignored God, things got worse for everybody.

In the brick shape write the name of your country's leader. Pray that they will not ignore God but listen to him.

Promises, promises

Have you ever made a serious promise (perhaps when you joined a group like Cubs or Brownies)? Can you still remember it?

Read Exodus 6:1–8.

God hadn't forgotten the covenant he'd made with his people (see 5 October). He had another message for them.

Draw arrows to the promises God made:

leave you in Egypt

turn away from you

I will

punish the Egyptians

be your God

rescue you and set you free

become angry with you

give you a new land

The promises God made would change the lives of the Israelites for ever. Have any of God's promises changed your life? How? Ask someone you trust at church the same question.

Thank you that you are our God who makes and keeps promises. Help me to trust them.

Nasties!

Long ago, the Egyptians got more than they bargained for when their king said he wouldn't obey God. The plagues just kept coming…

The River Nile turned to blood.

Frogs were everywhere.

Gnats swarmed.

Flies were in the palace and Egyptian houses, but not where the Israelites lived.

Livestock owned by the Egyptians mysteriously died, but the Israelites' livestock didn't.

Boils (painful sores) appeared on people and animals.

Hail hit people and animals and stripped trees. But it didn't happen to the Israelites.

Locusts completely covered the ground, eating trees and fruit.

Darkness lasted for three days in Egypt.

Every firstborn male died, but not those who followed God's rules for protection.

If you'd been there, would you think it was all just coincidence?

Doom!

10 November

God had said it was time for the Israelites to go free. But because the king wouldn't let them go, God sent plagues on Egypt. Each time a plague came, the king said the Israelites could leave, but then he changed his mind.

Read Exodus 11:1–7.

What did God say would happen when he sent the final plague (verse 1)?

What would happen to the Egyptians (verses 5–6)?

What would happen to the Israelites (verse 7)?

The king thought he could do what he liked and ignore what God said. Pray that the leaders of your country will know that God has final control, not them.

Blood on the doors

11 November

God had said that the oldest sons in every family in Egypt were going to die. What about the Israelites? Would their oldest sons die, too?

Read Exodus 12:21–28.

What saved those who believed what God had said? Fit the words into the grid.

doorpost   blood   honour   hyssop
Egypt   leave   lamb   spared

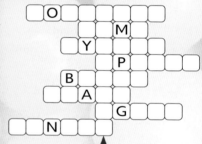

Every year they were to hold a festival to remember these things. What would the festival be called?
(Look above the arrow.)

What passed over at Passover?

When the Israelites heard that they were to be spared from death they worshipped God.

What's a good reason for you to worship God? Tell him now.

Dark night!

12 November

God is very patient and slow to get angry, but he doesn't put up with people going against him for ever. God had warned the Egyptians to let his people go. Every plague was a chance for them to see that God is the one true God. Would they believe in God this time?

Read Exodus 12:29–36.

Unjumble the sentences to tell the story:

Egypt was There crying loud in

_ _ _ _ _ / _ _ _ / _ _ _ _ /
_ _ _ _ _ _ / _ _ / _ _ _ _ _.

every Someone Egyptian dead home in was

_ _ _ _ _ _ _ / _ _ _ / _ _ _ _ /
_ _ /_ _ _ _ _ /
_ _ _ _ _ _ _ _/ _ _ _ _.

king country Leave now my The said

_ _ _ / _ _ _ _ / _ _ _ _, /
"_ _ _ _ _ / _ _ / _ _ _ _ _ _ _ /
/ _ _ _."

Lord God, thank you that all who believed you and did what you said were safe. Please help me to follow what you say.

Free at last!

13 November

Remember the word covenant? It's a two-way thing. God promises to be our God and we promise to be his people.

Read Exodus 12:37–42.

Link the answers to the questions:

How many men left?
Who went too?
What animals did they take?
What food did they take?
How many years had they been in Egypt?

430
Unleavened bread, without yeast
600,000
Women and children
Sheep, goats and cattle

God kept his promise and rescued his people from slavery in Egypt. His people were to show their promise to God by celebrating that night for ever.

Thank you, God, that we belong to each other. Please help me to be faithful to you, like you are to me.

Dear Dave

14 November

One of my friends had a really bad accident. Why did God let it happen? Love Emily

Dear Emily,
This is one of the biggest questions there is! Why does God allow bad things to happen? There is no easy answer. The Bible does tell us that God knows about suffering because that is what happened to Jesus. When Jesus was about to die he told his disciples to trust in God (**John 14:1**). They didn't understand but Jesus still wanted them to trust in him.

Sometimes bad things happen because someone does something deliberately wrong – the Bible word for this is "sin". The Bible tells us that the devil likes mucking things up, too. We can't blame God for evil because he doesn't do it!

Sometimes bad things happen and no one's to blame. But we can trust God to look after us, our friends and families.

Dave

No condemnation

15 November

We move from Egypt to Rome as we are now going to look at Paul's letter to the believers in Rome, the capital city of Italy. Can you find Rome on a map?

Read Romans 8:1–3.

If we're condemned we're sentenced to a punishment. Prisoners are condemned to stay in jail. If you don't do your homework you might be condemned to stay in and do it.

In a way, every person is condemned and deserves punishment because we've sinned. But Paul says that **f**or us there is no condemnation. **J**esus took our punishm**e**nt when he **d**ied, so we're n**o**t conde**m**ned when we're with him.

Copy down the bold letters to discover that God offers

_ _ _ _ _ _ _.

Jesus sets me free. Thank you, Lord!

Who's in control?

Have you ever played with a remote-controlled car?

Wouldn't it be odd if the car was in control of itself?

It might just crash into every obstacle, trip up all your family, escape from your house and disappear up the main road!

Read Romans 8:4–6.

Paul talks about two possible forces ruling or being in control of our lives. Hold this page up to a mirror to find out what they are...

Human nature   God's Spirit

Draw a wiggly line under the one that leads to a dead end.

Put a box around the one that leads to true life.

To have peace, which do we need to be controlled by?

Father God, thank you that you have given us your Holy Spirit to be with us and guide us throughout our lives.

Fully alive

Circle all the things that matter to you.

TV   hobbies   food   school
friends   holidays   music
sport   money

Something else?

Our lives are full of many things, but what actually rules your life?

Read Romans 8:7–11.

We have a choice! Let God's Spirit lead or go it alone.

Tick the results of having God's Spirit in your life and put a cross by the results of ignoring God. Check with the Bible verses.

- [ ] Can't please God.
- [ ] Fully alive.
- [ ] Dead because of sin.
- [ ] Life and peace.
- [ ] Pleasing to God.
- [ ] Don't belong to God.

Thank you for the way your Spirit makes us extra alive. Please help me not to let other things lead me, instead of the Spirit.

God on our side

Do you sometimes pick teams at school, perhaps for sport or group work? Who do you pick – the tallest, the fastest, the strongest, the most intelligent?

Read Romans 8:31–34.

Use these five words to complete the sentence below.

who God for be us

If _ _ _ is _ _ _ us, _ _ _ can _ _ against _ _ ?

What did God give us that shows that he will also give us many other good things (verse 32)?

Use the blank faces to draw your feelings:

When you are all alone, facing the opposition.

When you know that God is on your side.

Thank God for his love and support and for choosing you.

Superglue love

Has anyone in your house ever used superglue? It is very strong. You can glue a broken handle back onto a mug and it will never come off again.

Read Romans 8:35–39.

Paul lists some of the things that cannot separate us from God's love.

Check out verses 35 and 38 and circle the three items below that have been added to Paul's list

trouble   hardship   persecution

hunger   poverty   danger

death   angels   fierce

dogs   present   future

fast cars   old age

heavenly powers

God's love is like superglue – he loves us totally and completely, and nothing can separate us from that love.

Lord, it's so good to know that nothing can come between me and your love. Thank you!

Pouring out miracles

Adinda comes from Holland but she worked with Operation Mobilisation in England amongst homeless people.

Each night the team went out and gave people on the street a hot drink and some food.

One night they only had enough hot water left for one more drink so they decided to go home. As they were leaving they met a man who asked for a drink, so they made him one with the last of their water. Then he asked if his five friends could have one, too. Adinda trusted God and said, "Of course!" She poured each of his friends a hot drink. One person even asked for seconds. The hot water never ran out!

Be a kid!

Have you ever met anyone famous? What did they say to you? How did you feel?

Read Luke 18:15–17.

Jesus said, "The kingdom of God belongs to children like these". What did he mean?

Who does these things better? Write C (for children) or A (for adults).

trust people   accept gifts

earn money   drive a car

feel joyful   learn new stuff

forgive and make friends again

Put a * next to the ones you think are important to Jesus.

What does Jesus tell us to remember?

Fill the gaps with these words:

kingdom   never   enter   child

You will_____ get into God's_____ unless you _____ it like a _____.

Lord, thank you that I am very important to you.

Keep God's commands

🌀🌀🌀🌀🌀🌀🌀

22
November

Take two balloons (or draw them) and a soft felt-tip pen. On one balloon write "money".

On the other, write something that is important to you (like a computer, football or special clothes).

Blow up both balloons.

Read Luke 18:18–23.

What do you know about the rich man? Unjumble the letters:

He was a w i e h J s   a e l d r e.

He had obeyed the m n d e o a s t n c m m.

Did Jesus say that it's wrong to be rich? What did Jesus tell the rich man to do?

Unjumble the words:

you and the Sell the have

give all money poor to

Did he?

Is Jesus more important to you than the thing you wrote on the second balloon? If he is, burst that balloon (or tear up the paper). If not, talk to him honestly about it.

True riches

🌀🌀🌀🌀🌀🌀🌀

23
November

Remember the rich young man in yesterday's reading who wanted to be part of the kingdom of God? Find out how hard it was going to be for him.

Read Luke 18:24–30.

Join up the dots, then draw a needle.

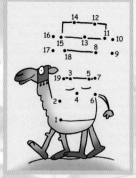

For the rich young man to be part of God's kingdom would be:

☐ Very, very hard

☐ Impossible

But if we put God first, what reward do we get? (See verses 29–30.)

Thank you, Lord, that you want the very best of everything for me. Help me to know what's important and what's not.

R U Blind?

Try to do these with your eyes closed:

Put your shoes and socks on. Write your name. Draw a circle. Work out what's going on around you.

Read Luke 18:35–43.

Underline the words that you think describe how the blind man felt.

curious	puzzled
eager	impatient
bored	determined
hopeful	tired

Match the two sides to explain what happened:

Ask	he followed Jesus, giving thanks
Believe	your faith has made you well
Receive	I want to see
Be grateful	he could see

Please Lord, help me to have a strong faith, like the blind man.

Zac meets Jesus

Here's a story you've probably heard.

See if you can spot something you didn't know before as you read it.

Read Luke 19:1–10.

Did you find something new?

If not, look again. Tell someone your new discovery.

Complete the story:

Zac was a little _ _ _ who collected _ _ _ _ _. He climbed a tree to see Jesus who said, "Hurry _ _ _ _." Zac did and _ _ _ _ _ _ _ _ Jesus with joy. He said he'd pay back the people he'd _ _ _ _ _ _ _ _ four times as _ _ _ _ . He also promised to give away _ _ _ _ his belongings. That proved that Zac was really _ _ _ _ _.

Lord, if there's anything you'd like me to change about the way I behave, please show me and help me.

174

It's all God's!

We all have things that we own – things that belong to us. Sometimes, we have to remind others that something is ours (although of course it's good to share our things!).

Read Psalm 24:1–2.

This circle represents the earth.

The earth and all that is in it belong to the Lord.

Now write or draw things that are in it – people you know, land, sea, animals, plants and so on.

Read aloud the words that are around the edge of the "earth".

Then complete this prayer:
Thank you, God, that _____
_____
_____
and _____
and _____(name the things you have written or drawn) belong to you. Amen.

Worship God

Get up and walk slowly around the room once. As you walk, imagine you live in Jerusalem long ago and are going up the hill to the Temple to worship God.

Read Psalm 24:3–6.

3 Who may climb the Lord's hill or stand in his holy temple?

4 Only those who do right for the right reasons, and don't worship idols or tell lies under oath.

5 The Lord God, who saves them, will bless and reward them,

6 because they worship and serve the God of Jacob.

Read the question in verse 3 again. To find the answer, underline the first five words of verse 4.

God will save us from the wrong things we do if we ask him to forgive us. Are there things you want to tell God that you are sorry for? Talk to him now and ask him to forgive you.

Make God welcome!

28 November

What's your favourite way of welcoming friends into your home? Some kids head for the computer games, while Mum might put the kettle on.

Read Psalm 24:7–10.

Welcome God into our lives? How?

When we're really sorry for the things we say, think or do we can ask God to forgive us. Then he comes into our life as our special friend and helps us to live his way.

Check out **1 John 1:9**.

If you really want God to forgive you, talk to him about it now. Then use some words from Psalm 24 to tell God how wonderful he is.

(Psst! If you want to know more about this, talk to a Christian grown-up you trust.)

Whose birthday?

29 November

No one is sure exactly when Jesus Christ was born and the Bible doesn't say. It probably wasn't when we celebrate it because that's the middle of winter in Bethlehem and it's unlikely that shepherds would have been out in the fields then.

So why do we celebrate Jesus' birthday on 25 December? The ancient Romans celebrated the shortest day on 25 December, in honour of Saturn, the god of farming. The ancient Babylonians had a big feast then, too, in honour of their god, Isis.

Christians didn't want to celebrate these gods, so some Christians used the holiday to celebrate the day their God came into the world. It became an official holiday of the Church about 300 years after Jesus was born.

At Christmas, shopping seems very important. A visitor from another planet might think that Christmas was a festival to the gods of money and shopping.

What do you think?

Stranger than fiction

Imagine: Everyone is sad that you have died, but you are really more alive and happier than ever, in another dimension!

Read 1 Thessalonians 4:13–14.

When we think about dying, we who belong to God don't have to be sad, like those who don't believe. God's quite capable of looking after those who belong to him, even when we die!

What difference does that make when you think about dying?

~~FEAR~~

Jesus died to forgive us and then rose again so that we can live with him for ever!

Do you think eternal life is too good to be true? Talk with God about it. Ask God to make your faith stronger.

Jesus is coming!

Before you read, think of a time when lots of exciting things were happening all around you.

Read 1 Thessalonians 4:15–16.

Lots will happen when Jesus returns. So much to see and hear.

Join to the eye what you'll see.
Join to the ear what you'll hear.

Jesus coming down from heaven
archangel's voice
believers rising to life
God's trumpet
a shout of command

Lord, thanks that you're coming back for me.

The world ends

Those who are still alive when Jesus returns are in for an adventure!

Read 1 Thessalonians 4:17–18.

So, whether we've died or we're still alive, when Jesus returns we'll all meet him together. Where?

_____

Verse 17 tells what happens after that. Rearrange the words and say it aloud.

with Lord we be forever the will

_ _ / _ _ _ _ / _ _ / _ _ _ _ /

_ _ _ / _ _ _ _ / _ _ _ _ _ _ _

Why not make a poster with these words on it? Ask if you can put it up in church to encourage everybody.
If you do, you'll be obeying verse 18.

Thank you, Lord, that we'll be with you for ever.

Unexpected

Do you really think Jesus might come back today?

Read 1 Thessalonians 5:1–4.

If you knew when a robber was coming, you'd lock the doors and windows.

What would you do if you expected Jesus to come back today?
Write or draw it here.

We know Jesus will return, even if we don't know exactly when.

(Only God knows that. Check out **Matthew 24:36**.)

Matthew 24:44 says Jesus will come when we're not expecting him.
What do you want to say to Jesus when he comes back? Tell him now.

Are you ready?

Imagine turning up for a music exam when you haven't practised, or for a sports final when you are hopelessly unfit.

How can we prepare for Jesus' return?

Read 1 Thessalonians 5:4–8.

How do we show we're ready for Jesus to return?

Fill in the missing vowels:

Wear f _ _ th _ nd l _ v _ like armour.

Wear th _ h _ p _ _ f s _ lv _ t _ _ n like a helmet.

Do these verses mean we should never sleep? No, they mean we have to live close to God, who is light, and stay away from "dark" things that are against God. If we live in God's light, we'll be ready when Jesus comes.

Dear Jesus, help me to be ready for your return.

Have courage

God chose you to be his very own. He has big plans for you! Think of a time when someone encouraged you to do something you thought you couldn't do.

Read 1 Thessalonians 5:9–11.

Can you find four things in these verses to give you courage?

We found these. Put exclamation marks after the one you think is the best.

God doesn't want to punish you

Instead he wants to save you

Jesus died for you, that's a fact

We'll live with him when he comes back

Who do you know that you can encourage? (It could be someone older or younger than you.) What could you say that will give them courage?

Please God, help me not to be shy to encourage others.

Dear Dave

6 December

How can I show Jesus that I love him this Christmas? Jenny

Dear Jenny,
Here are a few practical things you could do:

1 When you wake up on Christmas morning, say to Jesus, "Happy birthday Jesus, I love you!" That will make him really happy!

2 When you are getting ready for Christmas, try to remind your friends why they are celebrating.

3 If you have a special event at church, ask your friends to come and hear about Jesus.

4 Think of someone you could do something special for over the Christmas holidays.

5 Write a special little prayer that you could read at the beginning of your Christmas dinner.

6 Make, or buy, some fun cards which say something about the Christmas story.

7 Read Snapshots and the Bible every day during Advent. This will help you to be ready to worship Jesus at Christmas. And don't forget to pray!
Dave

All creation praises!

7 December

Read Psalm 19:1–6

Try reading this out loud. The sun is part of God's creation. What picture of the sun do these verses give? What do the heavens and the skies say about God?

Draw a picture based on these words. Use your picture to help you praise God.

Look out of your window. How many parts of God's creation can you see? Sky? Sun? Trees? Choose one part and tell God why you like it. Thank him for creating it. **Psalm 19:1** says the skies declare what he has done. What does the sky look like today? Draw it here.

With an adult you know well go on a praise walk. Ask a friend to join you. Stop whenever you see something wonderful that God has made. Praise him for making it.

God's words are good

Read Psalm 19:7–8.

Underline all the words that tell us what God's words, his instructions and commands are like.

"The Law of the Lord is perfect; it gives us new life. His teachings last for ever, and they give wisdom to ordinary people.

The Lord's instruction is right; it makes our hearts glad.

His commands shine brightly, and they give us light."

In the past some people called the Bible the "Good Book". Do you think this is a good name for it? Why?

Read the verses as a prayer. Say "Thank you, Lord" after each sentence.

God's words warn us

What's your favourite meal? Draw it here.

Psalm 19 says that doing what God says is even better than eating our favourite food!

Read Psalm 19:9–14.

Read verse 14 out loud. Make up some actions to go with the words.

God's words in the Bible tell us what he wants us to do. They also show us when we have let him down.

Sometimes we break God's rules without knowing it. At other times we do it deliberately. Use verses 12 and 13 as a prayer to say sorry to God.

God with Us

🗓 **10 December**

What does your name mean? Do you know why you were given it?

Read Isaiah 7:14.

Many people know the Christmas story well, but did you remember that Isaiah wrote this prophecy at least 600 years before the first Christmas? How did he know what to write?

One of Jesus' names is Immanuel. It means "God is with us".

Write some times when God is with you:

In bed
M
M
At school
N
U
E
L

Lord God, thank you for planning to send Jesus. Thank you that he is always with us.

What is he like?

🗓 **11 December**

Do you know anyone who's expecting a baby? What do you think the baby will be like?

Read Isaiah 9:6–7.

The Bible doesn't say what Jesus looked like, but it tells us about his character.

Draw your face and hair and write some words which describe you.

How does Isaiah describe what Jesus will be like?

W _ _ _ _ _ _ _ _
C _ _ _ _ _ _ _ _ _ _
M _ _ _ _ _ G _ _
E _ _ _ _ _ _ _ _ _ _ _ /
F _ _ _ _ _
P _ _ _ _ _ o _ P _ _ _ _

(Counsellor means adviser.)

Which of these names is most important to you? Why?

Thank Jesus for the name which means the most to you.

David's family

Do you know anything about your great grandparents? What were they like?

Read Isaiah 11:1–3. King

King David was Jesus' great great great (lots of greats)... grandfather!

David's family had good and bad members, but King Jesus was like a healthy new branch from a tree stump.

Write on the branches some of the skills Isaiah says a king needs.

Can you think of a time when Jesus didn't judge by appearances, but knew what people really needed?

Ask God to make the leader of your country wise, fair and skilful.

Our salvation

If two or three people all say the same thing, are you more likely to listen?

Read Jeremiah 23:5–6.

God told lots of different prophets that Jesus would come.

Jeremiah lived at least 500 years before Jesus. Can you find four things he said which were the same as Isaiah?

_____

_____

_____

_____

The Jews looked forward to a safe kingdom.
What can you do in a safe kingdom?

Jesus is our salvation because he saves us. What does he save us from?

Lord Jesus, thank you for saving me from...

Where was he born?

Do you live in a small town or a big city? Were you born there, or somewhere else?

Read Micah 5:2–5.

What does Micah say about Bethlehem?
You are one of the:

_____.

Out of you I will bring (or one of your people will be):

_____.

Look around the room and out of the window. Can you see…

a diary or calendar?

a map or picture of a town?

a piece of jewellery?

a plant or tree?

a baby or a mum?

How can these things remind you of God's plans for the first Christmas?

God made careful plans for Jesus. Thank him because he has good plans for you, too.

What kind of king?

Have you ever seen your country's leader riding a bicycle?

Read Zechariah 9:9.

You'd expect your leader to arrive in a posh car!

The Jews expected an army general, riding a war horse, but Jesus was a peaceful king. Can you think of a time when he rode a young donkey?

Complete the picture.

What can you rejoice about? Can you rejoice with your whole body?

jump	dance	cheer
shout	sing	grin
clap	wave	stretch

Is your country at war? Pray for God's wisdom for your leaders.

christmas abroad

16 December

What's Christmas like where you live?

Larrisa from Armidale, Australia

Christmas is in summer here. It's hot and it gets light very early on Christmas Day. Mums and dads don't like that much. The week before Christmas we have a barbecue outside in the church grounds. Some people dress up. After the sun goes down we sit on the grass and light candles and sing carols. We have Christmas parties outside, but it's really Jesus' birthday, not ours.

Sam, Caleb, Hannah, Micah and Josiah from Mozambique

It's hard to tell it's Christmas here. There are no decorations or trees or lights and no Christmas songs on the radio. We don't go to church but we get together with others and sing and pray and have Christmas lunch. We have meat and lots of salads because it's so warm – and Christmas pudding. The kids do Christmas plays and we all swap silly gifts. One day we hope that all the kids here will celebrate Jesus being born.

Dates matter!

17 December

What year were you born? What else happened that year?

Read Matthew 1:17.

History's important! Circle **T** (true) or **F** (false) for these statements. (Answers on page 192.)

The Olympics were held in Athens in 2004. **T/F**

A man first walked on the moon in 1999. **T/F**

There were four generations from Abraham to David. **T/F**

Hitler led Germany in the Second World War. **T/F**

Barack Obama is a rock musician. **T/F**

There were 28 generations from David to Jesus. **T/F**

Who's the oldest person in your family? Ask them what has changed since they were your age.

Lord, thank you that everyone's important to you, including me and my relative called _____ _____.

Like father, like son

18 December

Everyone has a dad, though you might not live with your dad, or even know him. But Jesus was different.

Read Matthew 1:18.

Mary became pregnant because God planned it that way. She didn't have sex. Remember what Micah prophesied 500 years earlier? (Look back to 14 December.)

Sally takes after her dad. They're both tall, thin and brainy. Draw them here:

Kevin takes after his dad. They're both short, strong and good at football. Draw them here:

Jesus takes after his heavenly Father, God. Think about something that Jesus did. What does it tell you about God?

Jesus = Saviour

19 December

Have you ever got completely the wrong idea about something?

Read Matthew 1:19–21.

It was a disgrace for Mary to be pregnant before she was married. Joseph got the wrong idea. He thought she'd had sex with another man.

What did he plan to do?

Draw a broken engagement ring in Joseph's thought bubble.

What did God tell him to do? Draw a wedding ring in the speech bubble.

"You will name the baby..."

JESUS

How do you think Joseph's feelings changed?

Thank you, Lord, that you always work out your plans perfectly.

Joseph's answer

Are you good at following instructions?

Read Matthew 1:22–25.

Joseph carried out God's instructions according to God's plan.

R	A	B	D	P	C	Q
M	N	M	A	R	Y	T
O	G	G	F	O	G	R
S	E	H	J	P	O	U
G	L	J	E	H	D	X
A	J	O	S	E	P	H
V	K	M	U	T	S	P
Y	W	Z	S	Y	P	N

There are six people in this story: God, Mary, Joseph, angel, prophet, Jesus. Find them in the wordsearch.

Why was each person important? Joseph is the star of this part of the story.

Unjumble the reason why.

He ybedoe _ _ _ _ _ _ God.

Lord, please help me to follow your instructions in the Bible.

Men from the east

Have you received any Christmas cards with a picture of the wise men on them?

Read Matthew 2:1–2.

What did the wise men ask? Write it in the star:

Match the questions and answers:

Who?   While Herod was king.

Where? Men from the east.

When?   By following a star.

Why?   In Jerusalem.

How?   To worship the new king.

Trick question: How many wise men were there? (Psst! Read carefully. This is the only place in the Bible they are mentioned.)

How can we worship? One way is to sing a song to God. Sing one now.

Which way?

22 December

Which way did the wise men go through Jerusalem to get to the palace and then on to Bethlehem?

The wise men followed the star because Jesus was special. They must have been very sure he was worth finding as they travelled 800 miles or more!

Thank you, God, that the star gave a sign that Jesus had come. Thank you for showing the wise men the way.

Herod wants to know

23 December

How would you feel in the presence of an angry king?

Read Matthew 2:3–6.

Draw Herod's angry face. Draw the teacher of the Law's face.

If you're reading with someone else, play a part each: H = Herod, T = teacher. If you're alone, play both parts, but use a mirror to check your expressions are different for each person.

H: Put on an angry, upset face and act the part of Herod. Give instructions to your advisers, and ask questions.

T: Put on a wise face and act as an adviser.

Answer Herod and try to calm him down.

Lord, although Herod was dangerous, danger is no problem to you. Thank you that you always protect me.

Happy christmas!

We hope you're having a good time this Christmas. But what about Herod? Was he enjoying things?

Read Matthew 2:7–8.

Complete the puzzle:

1 Herod was king of the _ _ _ _
2 He met the wise men in _ _ _ _ _ _ _
3 He wanted to know when they first saw the _ _ _ _
4 He sent them to _ _ _ _ _ _ _ _ _ _
5 He told them to _ _ _ _ for the baby
6 Bethlehem was in the land of _ _ _ _ _
7 Herod said he wanted to _ _ _ _ _ _ _ _ the baby Jesus.

(Answers on page 192)

1						*				
2										
3										
4			*							
5										
6						*				
7						*				

Circle a vertical word that says how Herod felt. Sort out the letters marked with a * to finish this sentence:
Herod was telling _ _ _ _.

Be near me, Lord Jesus; I ask you to stay close by me for ever and love me, I pray.

christmas presents

Did you get any Christmas presents? Which was your favourite? Why?

Read Matthew 2:9–11.

priest

Did you give any presents?
Did you choose carefully?
The visitors did.
king

Draw the three presents and find words to complete the sentences.

Gold for a _____.
A bottle of frankincense for a _____ when he prays
A pot of myrrh to put on a _____.

Which present is the strangest? Why do you think the wise men gave it? **dead person**

Lord, you give joy to everyone who meets you. Please help _____ to meet you.

Beware!

26 December

Do you remember your dreams?

Read Matthew 2:12.

God spoke to the visitors in a dream. What did he say?

Who else received God's instructions through a dream? (Psst! Look back to 19 December.)

Jerusalem

Bethlehem

Draw the visitors sleeping in their tent near Bethlehem, and draw Herod's palace in Jerusalem. Draw arrows to show which way the visitors went home.

Lord, thank you for the obedience of the wise men and all the people who obeyed you in the Christmas story.

Escape!

27 December

Have you ever been in real danger?

Read Matthew 2:13–15.

There are five mistakes in this story. Find them and correct them. Every time you find one, draw in a line of the pyramid.

An angel appeared in a dream to Mary. The angel said, "Isaiah is looking for the child. He wants to worship him. Take the child and his mother to Egypt. Stay there for a week." Joseph left at night. He stayed until Christmas. The prophet had said, "I called my son out of Egypt."

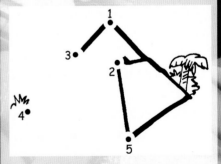

Pray for anyone you know who lives or works in a dangerous place.

Murder!

28 December

Have you watched the TV news recently?

Was it sad? Had anyone been killed?

Read about one of the saddest events in the Bible.

Read Matthew 2:16–18.

Use the words below to complete this lament. (A lament is a sad song.) You can sing it to the tune of "We three kings".

anything   sad

king   glad

Herod's this world's cruellest

_____.

Hear his jealous, angry voice ring

"Kill the baby boys and two-year-olds

Don't stop at _____."

Oh, Rachel's weeping, Rachel's

_____.

Herod's evil, mean and bad.

No more playing, joy or laughter,

Nothing now can make her

_____.

Pray for the families and friends of people who have been killed in recent fighting or accidents.

Back home!

29 December

If you were away from home for a long time, what would you miss?

Read Matthew 2:19–21.

What was the good news Joseph received?

What were his instructions? Fill in the missing vowels:

G _ t _ p, t _ k _ th _
ch _ ld _ nd h _ s
m _ th _ r, _ nd
g _ b _ ck t _ th _
l _ nd _ f _ sr _ _l.

Joseph must have felt encouraged. What can you do to encourage someone?

phone them

promise to pray for them

tell them something true, like "God has good plans for you"

lend them your things

anything else?

Pray for someone who needs encouragement.

A new start

Someone from London is a Londoner.
Someone from Sydney is a Sydneysider.

Is someone from Bamburgh a Bamburger?!

Where are you from?

Read Matthew 2:22–23.

Help Joseph, Mary and Jesus travel to Nazareth.

Nazareth

Joseph and Mary had a new start. The new year will soon be starting. Ask God to help you get to know him better next year.

Come and praise

God is so good.

Read Psalm 103:1–22.

Here are some of the reasons David gives for praising God. Can you find them in the puzzle?

K	M	E	R	C	I	F	U	L
I	N	M	B	C	J	O	S	P
N	R	O	D	V	U	R	E	A
D	E	R	W	T	S	G	V	T
H	E	A	L	S	T	I	O	I
A	S	D	F	G	H	V	L	E
P	R	O	M	I	S	E	S	N
U	Y	T	H	J	N	S	Z	T
O	S	T	C	E	T	O	R	P

kind	forgives
heals	protects
loves	merciful
patient	knows
just	promises

What reasons would you give to praise God? Tell him in any way you like – perhaps dance, sing or draw a praise picture.

Answers

11 January: all the statements are true

4 February: F; F; T; T; T

7 February: 200; 5; 2; 5,000; 12; 10,000

27 February: running

29 March: land, cities/towns, homes, wells, vineyards, olive orchards

2 May: jealous, conceited, proud, ill-mannered, selfish, irritable, record wrongs

17 May: all the statements are true

11 July: F; T; T; F; F; T

11 August: Silver, because it doesn't burn away

21 August: all the statements are true

6 September: 13 times

14 September: T; F; F; T; T

4 October: 150; 17th of the seventh; 40

26 October: T; F; F; T; T

1 November:

17 December: T; F; F; T; F; T

24 December: Jews; secret; star; Bethlehem; look; Judea; worship